Sunday Times best-selling author Vernon Coleman has sold over 2 million books in the UK alone. His books have been translated into 23 languages and sell in over 50 countries. His novels include *The Man Who Inherited a Golf course*, *The Village Cricket Tour*, *Deadline*, *It's Never Too Late* and the Bilbury series of novels.

CAT TALES

Cats have always played a big part in Vernon Coleman's life. This collection of anecdotes, essays and memories describes some of the cats he has known, and some of the ways in which they have affected his life and the lives of others. Vernon has resisted including stories which relate to cats performing tricks, in favour of the common thread which unites all of these tales — that in some way, someone's life was changed for the better, or was enriched, through knowing a cat.

Books by Vernon Coleman
Published by The House of Ulverscroft:

THE BILBURY CHRONICLES
BILBURY GRANGE
THE BILBURY REVELS
DEADLINE
BILBURY COUNTRY
IT'S NEVER TOO LATE
THE MAN WHO INHERITED A
GOLF COURSE
THE VILLAGE CRICKET TOUR
BILBURY PIE
AROUND THE WICKET
TOO MANY CLUBS AND NOT
ENOUGH BALLS

VERNON COLEMAN

CAT TALES

Complete and Unabridged

ULVERSCROFT
Leicester

First published in Great Britain in 2008 by
Chilton Designs
Barnstaple

First Large Print Edition
published 2009
by arrangement with
Chilton Designs
Barnstaple

British Library CIP Data

Coleman, Vernon.
 Cat tales.
 1. Cats- -Anecdotes. 2. Cat owners- -Anecdotes.
 3. Large type books.
 I. Title
 636.8–dc22

 ISBN 978–1–84782–930–6

Published by
F. A. Thorpe (Publishing)
Anstey, Leicestershire

Set by Words & Graphics Ltd.
Anstey, Leicestershire
Printed and bound in Great Britain by
T. J. International Ltd., Padstow, Cornwall

This book is printed on acid-free paper

To Donna Antoinette

Who has my heart
For safe keeping
All ways
And forever

Contents

Introduction

This book is about people whose lives have been changed by cats. Cats have always played a big part in my life. This collection of anecdotes, essays and memories describes some of the cats I have known, some of the ways in which they have affected my life and some of the ways in which they have affected the lives of others.

The stories in this book relate to incidents that happened to me, or that I observed myself. I have resisted the temptation to report stories which were told to me even if I heard them at first hand. When it comes to talking about cats some people can be inclined to exaggerate a little.

In particular, I have resisted including stories which tell of cats who have learned tricks such as managing to open a door by jumping up and catching hold of the handle. Such feats are entirely feasible (I've witnessed them myself) but they are neither exceptional nor worthy of recording. And they certainly don't change the lives of the people who know the cats involved.

The one thing most of these tales have in

common is that, in some way, someone's life was changed for the better, or was enriched, through knowing a cat. The effect cats can have on people can sometimes be slight and simple and sometimes subtle and complex. Unlike my book *Cat Fables*, there are, however, no lessons and no messages here. These stories are told simply for their own sake. I hope you enjoy them.

Vernon Coleman May 2008

PS The names of the people, and some of the cats, in this book have, with a few notable exceptions, been changed to protect their privacy. However, Alice, Thomasina, Dick, Harry and Timmy were the real names of very real cats.

PPS As is now traditional with my cat books this collection of stories is decorated with a selection of appropriate catoons. I did the drawings for *Alice's Diary* (my first cat book) because I didn't know any artists, didn't want anyone else (especially a stranger) to draw Alice and didn't want sophisticated artwork that would make Alice's words take second place. Since then readers have been kind enough to say that they like my squiggly drawings. And so the tradition continues in this, my tenth cat book.

The Cats Who Saved
A Bookshop

A few years ago two friends of mine, Bob and Mary, ran a second hand bookshop in the Cotswolds. In their previous lives he had been a journalist on a national newspaper and she had been a producer for a well-known, long running television programme. He was the one I knew best but I had met and worked with them both professionally.

They had run away from the rat race to find some peace, some space and a little time. His years in Fleet Street had given him high blood pressure and a two year history of angina. Her anxious afternoons and evenings at the television studios had left her with a stomach ulcer, irritable bowel syndrome and eczema. They had used their savings and the money they'd received from the sale of their London flat to purchase a bookshop and a tiny, thatched cottage less than a quarter of a mile away from it.

'I can walk to work!' Bob told me with great glee, when I visited to see how they were getting on. 'No more traffic jams. No more suffocating journeys on the Tube. I just tumble out of bed, have breakfast in the garden, and wander down to the shop to open at 10 a.m. on the dot when I'm there on time and a bit later when I'm not.'

They had stocked the shop with a mixture of their own books (he had written book reviews and had a huge collection of first editions), stock acquired from the previous owner of the shop and books bought by the crate from a London auction house. They'd supplemented this considerable stock with books bought by the armful from jumble sales, bring and buy sales and, a new phenomenon at the time, car boot sales.

'I don't mind selling a few disposable books — things bought for a holiday read,' said Bob. 'But we don't want to go too far downmarket. I'd like to acquire a good quality clientele — people interested in signed first editions.'

They had plenty of books and a pleasant old bookshop in which to display them (the shop was 18th century and the books were displayed in a series of book-lined rooms that were such a maze that it was easy to get lost in them) but there was one essential which was missing: customers.

The shop was in the high street of a small, much visited Cotswold village. On fine summer days thousands of people walked past their shop. But, by and large, that's what the potential customers did: they walked past. They didn't go into the bookshop and they certainly didn't spend any money.

★　★　★

'I don't think people are reading books any more,' Bob complained when I visited again after six weeks. The shop was looking rather sad and desperate. The two owners had gone downmarket in an attempt to attract some customers. Instead of containing an impressive looking collection of first editions the two bow-fronted windows now contained the usual colourful collection of remaindered cookery books, television tie-ins and biographies written by transient celebrities enjoying their few moments of undeserved fame. A battered old bookcase on the pavement outside the shop was stuffed with old books — all priced at 20 pence each.

My friend pulled out the exercise book in which he kept a list of the books he'd sold that week and read out the day's sales. 'A jacketless Book Club reprint of *Casino Royale* by Ian Fleming, a Barbara Cartland paperback, an old bound copy of the *Strand* magazine and a paperback copy of George

Orwell's *Animal Farm* which I sold to an American who, in a very loud voice, told me he had 3,000 acres in Texas and who clearly thought he'd just bought a book about a typical English farm.'

'I can't imagine the profit on those is going to put you into the top tax bracket,' I said.

'So far today the total takings amount to six pounds seventy pence. Without the *Strand* magazine we'd have taken one pound seventy.'

A grumpy looking man came into the shop clutching a paperback copy of a Jack Higgins novel. 'You've got this marked at 20 pence but there's a tear in the cover,' he complained. He held the book out and showed the tear to Bob.

My friend took the book from him, flicked through it and checked the back page. 'The book's all there,' he pointed out.

'The other books on sale don't have tears,' the man argued. 'And they're only 20 pence.'

'You're suggesting that I should knock something off for the tear?'

'Yes.'

'I'll knock a penny off,' said my friend. 'Nineteen pence. That's my best offer.'

The customer thought about this for a while and tutted loudly. Eventually he put his hand into his rear trouser pocket and pulled out a handful of change. He picked out two ten penny pieces and handed them over. My friend opened the till, took out a penny and handed the penny and the book to the customer. We watched as the man left, crossed the narrow, uneven pavement and climbed into a brand new Mercedes.

'Life running a bookshop is not quite how I'd imagined it would be like,' said my friend softly.

When I left, the next day, it was with a gloomy sense of foreboding. How long would my friends manage to survive? Did their bookshop dream really have a future?

The answer to the first question seemed to be 'probably not very long' and the answer to the second question seemed most likely to be 'no'.

They had not, I knew, ever expected to make a fortune from the shop. But they did need to earn a small living from it. Nothing extravagant — just a few thousand pounds a year.

* * *

Two months later I headed back in their direction again. It was Bob and Mary's wedding anniversary and I'd been invited to join a small party of friends celebrating the occasion. We were all booked into a local inn. I arrived a day early because I wanted to see how Bob and Mary were getting on with the bookshop.

'We're making money!' was Bob's first greeting when he met me at the railway station.

I congratulated him and threw my bag into the boot of his elderly Jaguar saloon.

'You wait until you see the shop,' he said, as he drove away from the station. 'We've got rid of the remaindered cookery books — gave them all to the local Church fete — and we've put all the 20 pence books into storage in a barn.' He explained that, unlike almost every other product, second hand books always rise in value over the years. 'Old paperbacks that cost two shillings and sixpence a few years ago now go for twenty pence,' Bob pointed out. 'That means that a book that originally cost twelve and a half pence now sells for twenty pence. If we keep those cheap books for another year or two they'll be selling for twice their current price. That's a pretty good rate of return.'

'I hadn't thought of it like that,' I told him. 'But the last time I was down here the 20 pence shelf seemed to be keeping you alive.'

'Ah, that was then,' said Bob. 'We've had a bit of luck since then.' He swerved to avoid a pothole and two boxes full of books on the back seat slid from one side of the car to the other.

'I'm pleased to hear it,' I told him.

'Mary's Great Aunt Thelma died,' said Bob. 'And although it doesn't sound nice to describe it as good fortune for us that's exactly what it turned out to be. She was 97 so I think she had a pretty good innings.'

'She left you some money? A mansion in Surrey and a yacht moored in the South of France?'

'Not a bit of it,' said Bob. 'I confess that we did have hopes but the dear old girl had been in a nursing home for the last eight years of her life and the fees had pretty well decimated her fortune. After the lawyer had taken his cut there was just about five hundred quid left. Mary had to cough up two thousand for the funeral costs.'

'So where did the good fortune come from?'

'Dear old Aunt Thelma had two cats,' explained Bob, turning into the driveway of the inn where I was staying and sliding to a halt about an inch away from a rhododendron bush. 'Presumably not valuable cats?' We got out of the car and Bob opened the boot. I removed my bag.

'Not a bit of it. A pair of common or

garden tortoiseshells called Ethel and Edna.'
He closed the boot lid and opened the rear
door of the car to reposition the boxes of
books that had been sliding around there.
'You settle into the hotel and come across to
the shop. I've got to take these books in.
We're running low on stock and Mary has
had me out scouring the countryside for
replacements. I picked these up from an old
Major before I met your train.'

* * *

After registering at the reception desk, and
depositing my bag in my room, I strolled
down the high street to Bob and Mary's shop.
    The shop's façade hadn't changed at all, of
course. The local planning officer would have
had a few words to say if it had. But instead
of looking rather sad and desperate the
bookshop had a prosperous look about it.
There were four people looking in at the
window and, as Bob had said, the selection of
remaindered hardbacks which had filled the
two bow fronted windows had gone and been
replaced by what seemed, even at a distance,
to be a fairly expensive selection of first
editions. I recognised a Sherlock Holmes first
and there were half a dozen fresh looking
jacketed hard backs by Graham Greene

— including a rare copy of *Brighton Rock*.

But it wasn't the books that the passers-by were looking at. They were admiring two cats which were curled up together right at the front of the left hand shop window.

I left the window shoppers on the pavement and wandered into the shop. Mary, standing behind the shop's tiny counter, was busy emptying one of the boxes that Bob had just delivered.

'Bob's just popped along to the vicar's,' apologised Mary. 'He's picking up a nice edition of *The Compleat Angler* that the vicar's brother wants to sell.'

'Things seem to have bucked up,' I said. I looked around. The shop was still dusty and rather untidy and there were books every-where. But I could see and hear people in the shop. It still looked like a proper second hand bookshop but it now looked like a prosperous second hand bookshop.

'It's all down to Ethel and Edna,' explained Mary.

I looked at her and frowned. 'The two cats?'

Mary nodded. 'My great aunt Thelma's cats. She had a lovely room in a nursing home just outside Oxford. They allowed her to keep the two cats in her room and when she died the cats came to me.'

'So Bob said. But no money unfortunately.'

'With nursing home fees of around a thousand a week there wasn't anything left,' said Mary. 'But our business started to boom the minute the cats came here.'

Just then the four people who had been standing outside the shop shuffled in. The two men both had to stoop to get through the low front door without banging their heads. 'We love your wonderful cats!' said the woman at the head of the quartet. 'Are they yours? What are their names?'

'Yes, they're ours. Their names are Edna and Ethel. Edna is the one with the little orange splodge just above her nose.'

'I noticed that you have some Graham Greenes in the window,' said one of the men. 'First editions?'

'They are,' said Mary.

'Do you have any American twentieth century firsts? Hemingway? Fitzgerald?'

'We've got a very nice *Great Gatsby* and a *Moveable Feast*,' said Mary. 'Both firsts and in decent jackets. We have some others too — though several don't have jackets. And we've got two Steinbecks and quite a good collection of Mailers.'

'Marvellous,' said the man.

'Go up the stairs and turn left. They're in the second room you come to,' Mary told

But it wasn't the books that the passers by were looking at. They were admiring two cats who were curled up together right at the front of the window.

him. 'If there's anything that takes your fancy bring it down with you.'

'Just like that?' said the man, surprised. 'No locked, glass-fronted cupboards?'

'Oh no,' smiled Mary.

They wandered off up the stairs. Ten minutes later they came back down again and bought nearly a thousand pounds worth of books.

'It's the cats,' Mary said, when they'd gone. 'People stop to look at them and then they come in to ask about them. And then nine times out of ten they start looking around. And two or three times out of ten they buy something. Not always something valuable, of course.'

'I don't suppose you stock books about cats, do you?' I asked. Mary laughed. 'Funny you should ask!' she said. 'I think we've got one or two of yours somewhere. I don't suppose you fancy signing a couple of first editions of *Alice's Diary* do you?'

The Cat Who Went To School

When I was six my parents bought me a cat for my birthday. He was a grey, long-haired cat and I loved him to bits. I called him Timmy. I cannot remember why. My night-time prayers were immediately extended, and Timmy was added to the list of close relatives and pets whose welfare I used to draw to God's attention as being worthy of his care and blessing. Timmy took his place behind my parents and just ahead of Tommy and Freddy. Tommy was a tortoise and try as I might I always found it difficult to feel great warmth towards him. Freddy was a huge gold-fish who inhabited a tank the size of a small swimming pool. The tank was kept out of doors and in winter my morning chores included breaking the ice on the top so that Freddy could breathe.

I suspect that Timmy leapt to this position of eminence in my prayers because I immediately recognised that although I was fond of Tommy and Freddy, I had a greater chance of developing a genuinely meaningful relationship with the grey ball of fluff who already enjoyed playing games with me, than with the tortoise, who seemed to spend much of the year hibernating, and whose most engaging characteristic when not hibernating was a mild affection for lettuce, or the goldfish, who, although he would swim to the top of his tank when he saw me approach, did so, I instinctively knew, only in anticipation of a sprinkling of fish food. I used to try feeding him more than anyone else but he never showed me more affection and never swam to the surface any quicker.

I lived around a mile and a half away from the school I attended and used to walk there by myself. I don't suppose many parents would allow their children to travel so far unattended these days but in those peaceful days of half a century ago the traffic was lighter and the perverts presumably too nervous to molest in daylight hours. My life might have appeared lonely (I was an only child) but I had the only child's vivid imagination and was never short of imaginary companions.

Timmy used to meet me on my way home. Every day he would be sitting on a garden wall about half a mile away from where we lived. He would see me coming, jump down off the wall, wait for me, rub against my legs and then trot along beside me, miaowing and rubbing and generally giving the clear impression that he was pretty darned pleased that I had decided to come back from wherever it was I'd been to.

He did this for three or four years.

And then I passed the eleven plus and changed schools.

The other children, awaiting the momentous move from junior school to grammar school were, I knew, worrying about making new friends, fitting in, coping with the homework and battling the older boys who had, it was rumoured, a scary variety of initiation tests prepared for the 'freshers' — the new boys. My sole worry, however, concerned Timmy. The new school I was about to attend was in the opposite direction to the junior school I was leaving.

As my first day at my new school approached I became increasingly concerned. My fear, obviously, was that Timmy would set off to meet me on my way home from my old school whereas I would be coming home from my new school. (It never occurred to me that he would not know when the school term had started. He had always managed to work this out for himself.)

What would happen? How long would he sit and wait for me? How long would it take me to run back home from my new school and to then set off towards my junior school

Timmy used to meet me on my way home.
Every day he would be sitting on a garden
wall about half a mile away from where we
lived.

so that I could meet him waiting for me?

I asked my mum to keep Timmy locked in when I started my new school.

But you can't keep a cat shut in when it has things it has to do. And Timmy, who somehow knew that I had gone back to school, was determined to escape. So when the brush salesman called (he lugged a huge suitcase around with him and my mother, who always had a soft spot for underdogs of any species, invariably answered the door in response to his jolly knock, and always bought a brush) Timmy slipped out.

I need not have worried.

Although I was now coming home from the opposite direction Timmy still met me; waiting on another garden wall half a mile away from home. He jumped down off the wall, rubbed against my legs and then trotted along beside me, miaowing and rubbing and miaowing and rubbing just the way he had when I'd been returning from primary school.

How did he know where to wait?

I have no idea.

It's just another cat mystery.

The Cat Who Played The Piano

As a boy, I lived on the edge of a town called Walsall in the West Midlands. A friend of mine called Peter, a boy of about my own age, had quite well-to-do parents and they lived in a house in a very smart part of the town. I can't remember what Peter's father did for a living or where their money came from but they always seemed to have plenty of it. Both Peter's parents had cars — his father a maroon coloured Ford Zephyr and his mother a yellow Ford Consul which had a black roof — and they had a double garage so that both cars could be kept protected from the elements. No one else I knew had a double garage. Every summer they spent two weeks touring on the continent.

Peter's parents were not musical or artistic in any way but they wanted their son to learn to play the piano. And so they bought him a brand new piano and hired a piano teacher to visit two evenings a week for half an hour and for a whole hour on Saturday mornings. (You can tell how unusual this was in the circles in which I grew up by the fact that I can still remember these trivial domestic arrangements.)

20

The piano teacher was foreign, very prim and ancient. Thinking back she was probably in her fifties. I have no idea where she came from but she spoke with a Germanic accent so I would imagine she was either German, Austrian or Swiss.

At the end of the Saturday piano lesson Peter's parents always expected to be treated to a short recital — some tangible proof that their son was benefiting from his no-doubt expensive musical education. When things went well the piano teacher would be rewarded with the knowledge that her lucrative appointment would be extended by at least another week and Peter would be rewarded with an extra two shillings pocket money. When added to his ten shillings a week pocket money the two shillings a week bonus he invariably received made him rich beyond my wildest dreams. My own pocket money was, at the time, half a crown a week and that enabled me to buy an entirely satisfying ration of comics and sweets, with enough left over to buy an occasional bottle of Dandelion and Burdock, and a packet of balsa wood once a month from the model making shop in the town centre. It seemed to me that twelve shillings a week would be enough to buy a house, run a motor car and hire servants to clean my bicycle and tidy my bedroom.

I was present at the Saturday recitals on more than one occasion because on Saturdays I would cycle round to Peter's home which, although situated in a much smarter part of town was no more than two miles away from my own, and wait for him to finish so that we could go off on adventures together. I was aged eight and he was nine at the time. We would put packed lunches into our saddlebags and ride off into the countryside where we would, according to the season and our inclination, sail homemade rafts, collect conkers, attempt (with absolutely no success) to catch fish with tackle consisting of a pea cane, a length of black cotton and a bent pin or simply try to hide from the bad men who were chasing us and who, in those halcyon days, existed only in our imaginations. (If it was raining we would play Monopoly on the dining room table or build balsa wood rafts for sailing on sunnier days.)

Whenever I was present for one of these piano recitals I would sit impatiently on the window seat wishing that Peter would play faster so that we could get outside sooner. I also wanted him to finish because I was looking forward to what was, for me, the main feature of the entertainment; the top of the musical bill.

At the end of Peter's effort there would be enthusiastic applause from his parents and myself while the piano teacher would smile, pat the bun at the back of her head and try to manage to look modest and proud at the same time. She didn't clap, of course, because if Peter had done well she was entitled to share in his glory.

And then, the moment Peter had finished, the family cat, a huge Persian called Gertie, would leap up onto the piano and stamp up and down the keys with great determination. She only ever did this when Peter had finished playing and was being fêted, applauded and, eventually, hugged, and she clearly did it in the knowledge that his prowess on the piano had attracted great approval and in the expectation that if she copied him she, too, would attract an equivalent amount of attention and approval.

The first time Gertie played the piano, Peter and I applauded ferociously and gave the cat a lot of fuss. The second time it happened Peter rushed into the kitchen, fetched a can of salmon, a dish and a fork and fed Gertie there and then on the floor beside the piano.

After that day, Gertie's recital became a weekly ritual and I used to make sure that I arrived in plenty of time to be there for her

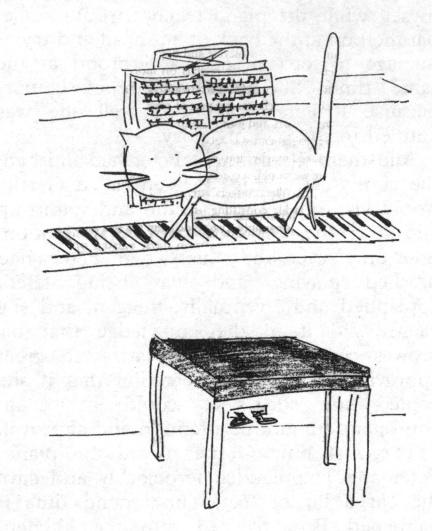

the family cat, a huge Persian called Gertie, would leap up onto the piano and stamp up and down on the keys with great determination.

performance. The fact that I had to endure Peter's performance was a small price to pay. (Despite his parents' determination and the hard work put in by his piano teacher Peter was not a naturally gifted player and this, combined with a total lack of interest in anything musical, meant that he never really made much progress.)

After a few weeks we became convinced that Gertie was making a genuine effort to play the piano, rather than merely walking up and down the keys. Even the piano teacher, who had regarded Gertie's first attempts as something approaching sacrilege, became convinced of this. Indeed, it seemed to me that it would have been hypocritical of her to smile with pride at Peter's clumsy efforts but to ignore the hardly less unmusical 'playing' of Gertie.

We had no tape recorder or home movie camera and so there is no record of Gertie's talent as a pianist. These days she would have been a television star: the piano playing cat.

But I don't mind that.

In my mind she played like a virtuoso.

And every time I remember her playing she plays with greater skill and more talent: her soft velvet paws hitting the keys with firm precision and creating real music magic.

The Missing Watch

When I was a medical student I spent a short weekend staying with a colleague called Harry who came from Yorkshire. His father was a country doctor and his mother the daughter of a hereditary peer who owned half of a county in southern England. Their family home was an impressive looking manor house that stood in about thirty acres of garden, private woodland and pasture. Their thirty acres was surrounded by farmland and moors. It was the first time I'd ever stayed in a house where you could not see another house from any of the windows. My friend's father was very proud of that and it was the first thing he told me when we met. He was so proud, indeed, that I suspect that if someone had erected a house on the horizon he would have blocked up all the windows from which the offending creation might be viewed.

Harry's parents were keen outdoor people and, within twenty minutes of arriving, the four of us (Harry and I and his parents) were in the garden clearing out a ditch that had become overgrown with brambles. Not having brought anything suitable with me I was lent a pair of Harry's Wellington boots and an old Barbour jacket that had last been waxed in about 1950. Harry's dog, a black Labrador called George, and the family cat, a gloriously lively black and white moggie called Patch, sat and watched.

It was during supper that Harry's mother noticed that her watch was missing. 'The strap has been loose for days,' she said, castigating herself.

'It must be in the ditch,' said Harry. 'We'll go out and find it after supper.' He turned to me and explained that the watch, a gold Rolex, had belonged to his grandmother and, as well as being valuable had enormous sentimental value.

And so at nine thirty that evening the four of us put our boots back on and drove the family's two Rovers (one a saloon and the other a Land Rover) onto the grass so that their headlights could illuminate the ditch while we searched for the missing watch. George and Patch came with us but this time, instead of just watching, they climbed down into the ditch with us. And, although it seemed unlikely (to say the least) that they had any idea what they were looking for, they scrambled around among the long grass, the nettles and the dock leaves looking for whatever it is they thought they should be looking for.

At ten minutes past midnight we gave up and went into the house. Harry's father poured us all a glass of whisky and we agreed that we would resume the search the following day. It wasn't quite the weekend in the country I'd envisaged but it was a weekend away from the medical school, the anatomy books and the pressure.

We sat beside a roaring log fire enjoying the aroma created by the sprigs of rosemary which Harry's mother had tossed onto the fire. We sipped our whisky and ate slices of bread, thickly cut from a freshly baked home made loaf. It was bread like no other I'd ever tasted. I ate it with a smear of tomato chutney and a chunk of cheese, and can still remember the taste. George lay on the hearthrug at Harry's feet, enjoying the warmth of the fire and the attention of his master.

At twenty past twelve we heard the slap of the catflap and Patch came padding into the room. In her mouth she held a dead field mouse, which she dropped onto the rug.

'She must have thought that was what we were looking for!' said Harry's father. He stood up, picked up the mouse and disappeared. Patch followed him.

'I tossed it back into the ditch,' he told us when he returned. 'Patch looked rather put out. Probably thought we'd be pleased and have it for supper.'

Fifteen minutes later Patch returned. This time she carried a small pipistrelle bat. This time her prey was still alive. Harry's father threw his jacket over it, wrapped it up and took it back outside. Patch followed.

Patch continued her hunt for whatever it was we had been looking for. At ten to one she came in with a small piece of rusty metal. None of us could identify it. Harry looked at Patch and shook his head. He took it outside and tossed it over the hedge. Patch followed him but stayed outside.

It was at twenty to two, just as Harry's mother decided that if she was going to be up for church at 8 a.m. she ought to be off to bed, that Patch came back into the house clutching something which shone and glittered in the flickering fire light. The cat was dishevelled and dirty and whatever she was carrying was clearly rather heavy for her.

Harry's father took it from her.

It was, of course, the missing Rolex.

We all stroked her and then Harry's mother, followed by Patch, went off to the

In her mouth Patch held a dead fieldmouse,
which she dropped onto the rug.

kitchen. 'I gave her a tin of sardines,' she announced. 'And a dish of fresh cream.'

'Very fair reward,' agreed Harry's father.

George the Labrador lifted his head, opened an eye, yawned and went back to sleep.

Cloudio's Victory

I once lived next door to a couple who shared their home with a small and very noisy Jack Russell terrier called Rex (quite inappropriately) and a large and outwardly quite serene white Persian called (quite appropriately) Cloudio. My neighbours were both solicitors.

The cat loved nothing better than to doze in the sunshine. The dog loved nothing better than to bark at the cat and, occasionally, to try to attack it. (These attacks were invariably fruitless for the cat was twice the size of the dog and would respond with a flash of claw and a terrifying snarly hiss. But the attacks were, nevertheless clearly annoying.)

I was fortunate enough to be sitting in my garden when Cloudio finally shut Rex up and stopped him bothering her.

It was my neighbours' habit to go for a drive in the country on Sunday afternoons, and to stop somewhere and take Rex for a good, long walk.

And so one Sunday afternoon, Rex was duly sitting in the car, waiting for his master and mistress to drive off to somewhere in the country.

Unfortunately for him they had been kept indoors by a telephone call.

Cloudio spotted this heaven sent opportunity and purred with delight. Even ten yards away, on the other side of the fence, I could hear her purring and I could see what was going to happen long before it happened.

First of all Cloudio climbed onto the car bonnet. And sat there. In full view of Rex.

Now, Rex regarded the car as his territory. He was the only one of them who was allowed into the car and actually taken out in it. And to see Cloudio sitting on the bonnet was more than he could bear. He leapt up and down and barked and yapped and yelped and, of course, it was all to no avail because he was on the inside and Cloudio was on the outside.

Cloudio then went up onto the roof.

Rex, who knew the cat was up there somewhere but couldn't see her, was driven even madder with rage. He barked and jumped up and down and tore at the seats with his claws and his teeth in his rage.

Then Cloudio went onto the boot of the car.

And so Rex went into the back of the car and started biting and tearing and yapping and making a terrible noise and an even more terrible mess.

Cloudio then went up onto the car roof.

Being a good neighbour I called out. But no one heard me. They were busy with their telephone call. And I confess that I was on the cat's side in all this. I didn't call too loudly.

Finally, my neighbours emerged from the house. Cloudio, who had seen them coming, leapt off the car and disappeared across the lawn to her favourite spot beside the summerhouse. Rex, who could no longer see Cloudio and who did not realise that his owners were coming, kept on yapping and barking and tearing and biting the upholstery.

The two solicitors were not amused.

And as the car drove away I could hear them shouting at Rex as first one and then the other spotted the damage he had done.

When they'd disappeared, I wandered over to the fence from where I could see Cloudio more clearly. I called her name. She raised her head, opened one eye and, I swear, she smiled at me. I smiled back. 'Congratulations,' I murmured. I then went back to my deckchair and my book.

From that day on Rex left Cloudio alone. He would walk past her as though she wasn't there. He didn't bark at her. He didn't trouble her at all. He was thoroughly, completely, utterly defeated.

The score, as it so often is, was Cat 1 Dog 0.

The Matchmaker

When I was in the sixth form at school, a man called Alec Dickson came to talk to us about an organisation he had set up called Community Service Volunteers (CSV). He was a retired colonial administrator and a few years earlier he'd founded another organisation called Voluntary Service Overseas (VSO). VSO sent British school leavers and young graduates to work in Third World countries for a few months or a year — either between leaving school and attending university or immediately after graduating. The organisation became hugely successful but for various reasons which I don't entirely understand, and which don't matter here, Alec had decided that there was a need for something similar but less exotic rather closer to home.

And so he founded CSV.

When I met him he'd only just started and had recruited no more than a handful of volunteers. They were, I think, all school leavers who hadn't yet got jobs, hadn't decided what to do with their lives or were waiting to go to college or university.

No one else at school with me was in the slightest bit interested. The majority were ready to go to university and they couldn't wait to get there. They didn't want to take a year out and mess around. They were in the learning groove and they wanted to stay there.

I was the only one who volunteered to join CSV and I'm not entirely sure why I did. I was, I suspect, tired of learning stuff which didn't seem to me to have much relevance to real life, tired of cramming for examinations and ready to see some real life. I had five years studying ahead of me at medical school and I wanted a change. I'd chosen to study medicine because the idea of being able to help people appealed to me but it seemed pretty clear that if I went straight to Birmingham to study medicine it would be some time before I was in a fit state to be of any real use to anyone. The University agreed to keep the place for me and to let me spend twelve months learning a little bit more about life.

And so off I went to the new town of Kirkby on the outskirts of Liverpool. An innocent grammar school boy in a blazer, grey flannels, white shirt and school tie.

This was in the early 1960s and Kirkby had been widely described as the toughest town in

Britain. The local police station had metal grills over all its windows and barbed wire along its walls and it looked like a fortress. Actually, it didn't just look like a fortress — it was a fortress. At night, buses which travelled from Liverpool to Kirkby only did so when they were followed by a police car containing two officers.

I had a room at the local vicarage, an oasis of middle-class peace among a desert of crumbling council houses, smashed up telephone boxes, boarded up shops and roadways littered with glass and half bricks. Alec Dickson had arranged that I would take my meals with the vicar and his curate. I had thirty shillings a week pocket money to cover clothes, transport and all other expenses.

And so on Monday morning, without any idea of what I was doing (or how I would do it) I put on my school clothes and set off to change the world.

Most of what happened next is another story for another time, but not all of it.

My role in Liverpool had never been strictly defined. Alec Dickson told me that my job was to be a catalyst — 'to make things happen'. The idea of sending an undeniably callow youth into one of the toughest areas in Britain, where robbery with violence was more the social norm than voluntary service, was, on reflection, bordering on the absurd. I doubt if health and safety regulations would allow it to happen in 21st century Britain.

From the start it seemed to me that I had two choices. I could either spend my year in Liverpool helping old ladies across the road or I could spend my time trying to teach people to help one another. (Put baldly this probably sounds extraordinarily patronising, but this, remember, was 1964, and I was eighteen and brimming with good intentions. Anyone who doubts my innocence should know that for the first month I wandered around the most dangerous town in Britain wearing a Grammar school uniform. I held my comb under the tap every morning so that I could get a good parting. In retrospect, I firmly believe that the only reason I survived the first month was that I was regarded as too eccentric, too strange, to be a worthwhile target for a half brick or a whack with a piece of lead pipe.)

Clearly, if I was going to get anything done I needed three things: volunteers, something useful for them to do and probably some money or sponsorship.

Not having the foggiest idea what I could or should do I wandered around trying to get my bearings. I soon got lost and found myself on the local industrial estate. The biggest factory I could find manufactured paint. I tottered in and asked to speak to someone.

'Who do you want to speak to?'

'Er, I don't really know.'

'What do you want, son?'

'I'm, er not quite sure.'

In the end I left with the promise of a large supply of paint. The tins were, I suspect, left over discontinued colours. But I neither knew nor cared. I had a seemingly inexhaustible supply of paint. Now all I needed was something to paint and someone to do the painting.

I visited the local Citizens Advice Bureau.

'Is there anything in town that needs painting?'

'There are hundreds of pensioners living in really grubby council flats.'

So I started knocking on doors asking anyone who seemed old if they wanted anything painting.

And finding courage from somewhere I contacted all the local schools and asked if I could speak at their morning assemblies. To my horror and astonishment I was given permission. I told the kids I was looking for people to help paint old people's flats. With nothing much to do except throw half bricks at one another a surprising number of school pupils put their hands up.

I sent the keenest (some as young as twelve) wandering around the town knocking on doors and making a survey to find out where the old or disabled people lived. None, I'm pleased to say, were kidnapped or locked in cellars.

I had the three things I needed: something to do, people to do it and stuff to do it with.

I then had two huge strokes of luck.

First, the local Meals on Wheels group, discovering my presence and finding out that I had a driving licence (not all that usual among 18-year-olds in the early 1960s), enrolled me to drive their beaten up old van around the town to deliver meals to the hungry, elderly and housebound. In return, they allowed me occasional use of the van at other times of the day. The van would not have passed a modern MOT test (I doubt if it would have satisfied EU requirements for scrap) but if it was always parked facing downhill it was surprisingly reliable and it had a huge capacity. I found that I could cram an awful lot of paint and a good many kids into the back of it.

Second, I don't know who told them but the council found out what I was doing. The council bureaucrats were not well pleased. Firm suggestions were made that painting council property might be against the law.

Questions were asked. The local newspapers ran stories.

And then the unions got interested. Painting flats was taking away work from their members. There was outrage. No one had been planning to paint the flats. The council wasn't prepared to pay for the paint or the labour. And the union members weren't going to lose any work. But there was much indignation.

It was, to my surprise, precisely what I needed for my painting project to take off. When I warned pupils at one school that what I was asking them to do might get them into trouble with the council, every single pupil volunteered. The idea of doing something that wasn't approved by important adults appealed to them. Kids love doing things that aren't allowed. Most people who volunteer for anything have to get something out of it for themselves. That's human nature. They might not know this, and they might not know what it is they want, they need or they're getting, but it is, nevertheless, true.

The result was that I soon had surprisingly eager schoolchildren painting flats at evenings, at weekends and during their holidays. The Meals on Wheels van was running around the town almost full time, dropping off volunteers and paint. It spluttered and sighed and made a good many strange noises but it never let me down as long as I always remembered to park it facing downwards on a decent hill.

And this (thank you for your patience) is where the cat comes into the story.

One of the old ladies whose flats was being decorated, a sweet soul with the slightly improbable name of Emily Postlethwaite, had a cat. The cat, a much-spoilt long-haired lap cat, who was called Ernie in memory of Emily's brother who had died in the trenches in the First World War, didn't like the smell of paint. And he probably didn't much care for the influx of noisy, paintbrush wielding teenagers either. And so, as cats will do when they feel inconvenienced in any way, he bolted. Emily, who lived alone and who knew no-one in the area, was heartbroken. Ernie was, in many ways, her life. Emily had no relatives left alive and had made no friends. She and Ernie lived on the sixth floor of a multi storey block of flats and, since the lift only worked intermittently, there she stayed. Marooned on a small desert island high in the sky.

This was my first disaster. My first unhappy 'customer'. I was devastated. It was all my fault. I had ruined the life of a 77-year-old woman. I immediately pulled together as many of my helpers as I could (in a town ruled by gangs and gang leaders I had by now acquired a surprisingly large army of neophyte painters and decorators) and began a search of the neighbourhood. At first it seemed impossible that such a fat and out of condition cat should have managed to run down six flights of stairs and disappear into the urban jungle at ground level but when we failed to find him it seemed that that was exactly what had happened.

Alerted by the sound of schoolchildren running here, there and everywhere yelling 'Ernie!' and 'Here, pussy! Puss, puss!' Emily's neighbours stuck their heads out of their front doors to see what was going on. All, without exception, were keen to help when they heard what had happened.

And it was one of the neighbours, a 79-year-old retired dockyard worker called Jack McBride, who came up trumps. He lived on the seventh floor, a floor higher than Emily, and had opened his front door on the evening of Ernie's disappearance to find the escapee asleep on his front doormat. Being a kindly man he took the cat into his tiny flat and gave it a saucer of milk and a small piece of fish he'd been keeping for his supper. We had concentrated our efforts on the floors below Emily's flat. He, living above, had not heard the commotion we had been making as we continued our search.

Since her flat still stank of paint I escorted Emily upstairs so that she and Ernie could be reunited. Both were undoubtedly pleased at this reconciliation, though I have to say that Ernie, full of milk and fish, seemed to put less into the reunion than Emily, who had been so heartbroken that she hadn't had a thing to eat all day.

Jack invited Emily to stay with him while the painting continued. Emily, keen to stay with Ernie, and knowing that if she took him back downstairs he would probably run away again, gladly accepted. Jack had a small spare bedroom and while he made up the bed I went back downstairs and fetched the few things Emily said she needed. She trusted me with the key to her flat. Since it was full of her treasures, and everything in the world that she owned, this was a greater sign of trust than I realised at the time and was, perhaps, more a sign of the times than a sign of my particular trustworthiness.

By the time my teenager painters had finished redecorating her flat, Emily and Jack were getting on well together. They had, they discovered, a good deal in common. Both loved natural history programmes on the television, both were keen card players and both loved cats in general and Ernie in particular. I became friends with all three of them.

A month after we had finished the painting and Miss Postlethwaite had moved back into her flat I called round to see how she and Ernie were getting on. I found Mr McBride sitting at her dining room table. He and Miss Postlethwaite were playing poker, using buttons for money, and Miss Postlethwaite was, she told me with considerable delight, three million pounds ahead. I was invited to join in and was given a supply of buttons to start me off. When I left, an hour and a half later, I was down half a million pounds.

Five months after that, having decided that at their time of life a long courtship was giving fate too much of a chance to interfere in things, I got an invitation card telling me that Miss Postlethwaite was marrying Mr McBride and that I would be a very welcome guest at the church and the reception afterwards. 'Come to the wedding and we'll forget about the £500,000 you owe,' was scribbled on the bottom of the card in bright blue ink. Two of the girls who had helped paint Miss Postlethwaite's flat were acting as bridesmaids and the rest of the gang would attend and form an arch outside the church, with raised paint brushes replacing the more

46

Miss Postlethwaite was marrying Mr McBride.

usual display of ceremonial swords.

I was at medical school by then but I skipped a couple of anatomy lectures and went to the wedding. Even without the £500,000 bribe I wouldn't have missed it for the world.

The newly married couple were, they told me, moving into Mrs McBride's apartment. 'It's much smarter than my place now that it's been repainted,' explained the groom.

I asked if they were going on a honeymoon.

'Oh no,' they replied together.

'We couldn't leave Ernie,' explained the bride. 'He wouldn't like it.'

The Cat Who Didn't Like Opera

When I was at medical school in Birmingham I shared a flat with three other medical students. We had the whole of the top floor of a huge, detached Victorian house in a rather smart part of Edgbaston. The flat was so large that we used to have bicycle races indoors.

The woman next door was an opera singer and every morning she practised her scales. Even though her house was fifty feet away I could hear her if I opened my window. It was an extraordinary sound and the exercises, up and down, down and up, up and down, seemed to last for hours.

One day we found a grey Siamese cat wandering around in our flat. It had come in through the front door (which we only ever shut in really cold weather — we were all over six foot tall and had nothing whatsoever worth stealing so we had no fear of thieves) and climbed the stairs.

We didn't know where it had come from so we fed it and let it stay. It was, we discovered, exceedingly fond of pilchards. Later that evening a stout, red-faced man huffed and puffed up our stairs and demanded, very loudly, to know if we'd seen his wife's cat. He was, it seemed, the husband of the opera singer and the cat belonged to her (insofar as any cat can ever 'belong' to a human being). The cat was, he told us, an expensive present sent to his wife by a fan who happened to be a cat breeder. We gave him the cat, which seemed unhappy at leaving us, and he huffed and puffed back down the stairs with it in his arms.

This happened every day for the following week.

The cat would arrive with us in the morning and the husband would pick it up from our flat later in the day. We tried to take it back once but their front gate was locked and no one answered when we rang the bell.

It was on the third day that I realised that the cat was arriving just after the opera singer had started her morning vocal exercises. And, from the cat's behaviour, it was pretty obvious that the cat wasn't much taken with the noise she made. When the cat arrived in our flat it would head straight for the rooms that were furthest away from the side of the house where the opera singer was our neighbour.

I mentioned this to the fat man.

'I don't think the cat much likes your wife's singing,' I told him. It wasn't the most tactful remark I've ever made. In a lifetime of unintentional tactlessness it is probably quite high on the list. Just above telling the truth when a woman I knew asked if I liked her new dress and just below asking a famously irascible newspaper editor if his lack of height explained his constantly apparent inferiority complex and consequent aggression.

'My wife is one of the highest paid singers in Europe!' he told me indignantly.

'Maybe the cat isn't a keen opera fan,' I suggested, helpfully.

'It's a Siamese cat!' snorted the husband derisively. People are always said to snort derisively, but he really did. 'Siamese cats are exceptionally intelligent and well bred. Of course he will like opera.'

I gave up and handed the cat back.

'And please don't feed it fish,' he told me, over his shoulder. 'Fish makes the cat's breath smell.'

After three weeks of this the opera singer and her husband gave up. They did try to keep the cat in on two mornings but on both occasions the cat proved too good for them.

'You'd better keep the damned cat,' said the husband one evening. 'I'm not fetching it back again.' He glowered at the cat which was

51

curling itself between my legs. 'We did think of selling it but to be honest it's more trouble than it's worth.'

And so we acquired a cat. We called her Sophie.

Three weeks later the enormously well bred and exceedingly expensive Siamese cat gave birth to kittens. And, judging by their colouring, it wasn't difficult to see that this had not been an arranged coupling.

There were plenty of cosy cupboards and dark corners available to her but Sophie, now a new mother, gave birth in the bath which she then proceeded to use as a playpen. (The bathroom was as far away from the opera singer's house as it was possible to get.)

When she wanted her kittens to do a little exploring she would pick them up, one at a time, by the scruff of the neck and jump out of the bath with each one in turn. Without her help the kittens could not climb out of the bath. For six weeks we had to manage without a bath. It wasn't a great hardship. We either used to sneak into a shower room at the Queen Elizabeth hospital or, since a medical student we knew well was going steady with a nurse, we would use the bathroom in the nurses' home when we felt that we needed to clean up a bit. (We weren't supposed to enter the nurses' home at all but

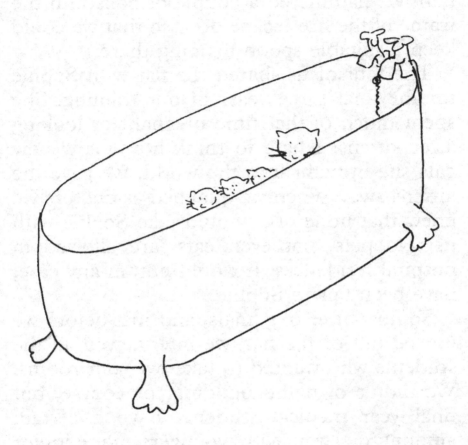

Sophie gave birth in the bath which she then proceeded to use as a play pen.

the fire escape door could easily be opened from outside if you had a dessert spoon handy. During the cat's occupation of our bath we hammered a couple of nails into the frame of the fire escape door so that we could keep a suitable spoon hanging there.)

The four of us shared the flat with Sophie for the final three years of our training. She spent much of that time pregnant or looking after kittens. I hate to think how many new cats she brought into the world. We gave the kittens away. When we qualified as doctors we knew that none of us could take Sophie with us. No pets, not even cats, are allowed in hospital residences. It would not, in any case, have been fair to Sophie.

So, just after our finals, and just before we moved out of the flat, we interviewed all the students who wanted to take over our rooms. We didn't own the building, of course, but final year medical students have a certain amount of sway with younger, more junior students (or, at least, they did in those days) and we made it pretty clear that we weren't going to let anyone take over the flat if they weren't also prepared to take on the responsibility for looking after Sophie. Handing over the bath when it was needed was one of the requirements that was beyond negotiation.

Eight years later I was back in Birmingham for a few weeks to make a television series. On the morning of my third day there I told the taxi driver who was taking me from my hotel to the television studios to make a small detour so that I could call in at our old flat.

The front door was open and no one answered when I called out. So I raced up the stairs to the bathroom in the vague hope that Sophie might be there.

She was.

She was lying in the bath with four kittens beside her.

As I got back into the taxi to continue my journey I stopped for a moment to listen to a familiar sound.

'Who or what is making that racket?' demanded the taxi driver.

'It's an opera singer,' I told him. 'Practising her scales.'

'I wouldn't like to live with that,' muttered the taxi driver.

I smiled.

Nor had Sophie.

The Cat Who Liked
Gardening

I spent six months working as a house physician at a hospital in a town on the south coast of England, to the west of Brighton.

Towards the end of my contract one of the consultants for whom I worked invited me to lunch. This wasn't anything special. I wasn't his favourite. It wasn't a 'treat'. The consultant, recognised as an eminent physician in his field, but regarded by the staff as the thin, rather mean man he appeared to be, used to invite all his house physicians to lunch. It was offered as a payment for all the times we'd helped look after his private patients. It was not, to be perfectly honest, much of a reward. Other consultants would quietly hand their housemen a bottle of claret or, so rumour had it, a crisp ten pound note sealed in an envelope. The consultant I worked for offered lunch. It was a semi-royal invitation which is to say that it did not allow for a refusal. To add insult to injury the invitee was, I had been informed by the consultant's secretary, expected to take along a bottle of wine.

Having lunch at the consultant's house (which involved two lengthy bus rides) wasn't the way I would have chosen to spend my free time. In those days it wasn't at all unusual for junior hospital doctors to work over a hundred hours in a week. Several weeks, when the doctor who covered for me was away sick, I actually worked or was on call for 168 hours. Three or four hours away from the hospital were valuable. My plan was to get away as soon as lunch was over and, if there was still time, take the bus to Brighton where I intended to sit on the pier and allow a warm sea breeze to wash away the smell of hospital which, I knew, enveloped me like a shroud.

Lunch was a dreary affair. The consultant's wife, as thin and apparently as mean as her husband, served very small portions and didn't offer seconds. The potatoes were allegedly mashed but in reality they came from a packet and hadn't seen a fork until they arrived at the table. The cabbage and the carrots were overcooked and watery. For pudding we had a slice of frozen treacle tart which was served luke-warm and with a thin coating of lumpy custard. The bottle of supermarket wine that I had taken with me had disappeared into the kitchen, presumably to be kept for a more illustrious guest. The meal made me realise that the food served in the doctors' mess at the hospital wasn't all that bad. The cook working in the mess did at least serve decent portions.

'Would you like to see the garden?' asked the consultant when his wife stood and began to clear away the custard-smeared plates.

Without waiting for an answer he opened the French windows and stepped out onto the small patio which separated the house from the garden. I followed. As we did so we were joined by a mackerel tabby which had been resting on a wooden bench a few yards to the left of the French windows. The three of us headed up a crazy paving path which led away from the house and across a neatly trimmed lawn.

'I grow my own vegetables,' said the consultant, over his shoulder. 'Fresher, better tasting and much cheaper than the stuff you get from the shops.'

He led me to a small area of garden which had been dug over and turned into a busy little vegetable patch. The cat, which had followed us, jumped up into a wheelbarrow and sat down.

'You can help me plant some more peas,' he said. 'Do you good. Fresh air and gentle exercise. You chaps spend too much time shut away in the hospital.' He took a bunch of keys from his pocket, selected one and unfastened the padlock on a small wooden shed. He opened the door and took out a spade. 'Just dig over that stretch of earth,' he told me. He patted his pockets. 'Damn,' he said. 'Forgotten the seeds. I'll pop back and fetch them.'

He disappeared back down the path to the house leaving me to dig his garden.

'Splendid!' he said, when he returned half an hour later, brandishing an unopened packet of seeds. His breath smelt of brandy and I guessed that he'd taken me up the garden and then nipped back down again so that he could have his after lunch snifter without having to offer me a glass. He popped into his shed, found a wooden dibber and started to prepare the ground for his seeds.

The moment he did this the cat jumped out of the wheelbarrow and wandered over towards him. And then, to my astonishment, as the consultant started making a trench for the seeds, the cat started to help. The consultant saw me watching. 'The cat always helps,' he told me. As the consultant created his trench the cat, starting a few feet away, created a trench of his own. At first I naturally thought that the cat was preparing a trench to satisfy some natural needs of its own. But it wasn't. When the two of them had finished preparing their shallow trenches the

'I expect you'll want to be getting back,' the consultant said.

consultant tore the top from the packet and, after making rude comments about the number of seeds supplied, began to sow what was available into the trenches which he and the cat had made. The cat, working behind him, covered up the seeds with fresh earth. It was quite extraordinary to watch. The consultant sowed and the cat covered up.

'Splendid!' said the consultant when the two of them had finished. He stood up, admired what they had done together and beamed at me. 'I expect you'll want to be getting back,' he said. I'd done my digging and he didn't need me any more. He looked at his watch. 'There's a bus in ten minutes from the stop just along the road.'

The added surprise was that the consultant didn't seem in the slightest bit astonished at what the cat had done. It seemed normal to him and he just took it for granted.

But for me, watching that amazing cat help sow a row of peas was well worth the long bus ride, the miserable company and the lumpy custard. In fact, if it wasn't for that cat, the only feline gardener I've ever met, I would, by now, have doubtless forgotten all about the consultant and his unwanted luncheon invitation.

The Music Loving Cat

A friend of mine, whose identity I will protect by calling him Jim, laboured under the misapprehension that he had a good singing voice. He would sing anything (show tunes, pop songs, snatches of opera, hymns, Christmas carols, folk songs) but whatever he chose to sing he would always sing it loudly.

His family and friends tried to persuade him to take up some other interest. Stamp collecting was one of the favourites. A cousin suggested that bell ringing would be more socially acceptable. An uncle recommended that he take up yodelling.

But Jim persisted. And whatever he sang he continued to sing loudly. He genuinely believed that he had a wonderful voice and that he had a duty to share his talent with those around him.

And then his wife bought a cat for their children.

The cat soon made it clear that it didn't think much of Jim's voice.

Every time Jim started singing the cat would jump upon his shoulders, reach round

Every time Jim started singing the cat would jump upon his shoulders, reach around and gently but firmly place a paw against his lips.

and gently but firmly place a paw against his lips.

Jim soon got the message.

'If even the cat can't stand my singing I suppose I'd better stop,' he admitted.

Family and friends clubbed together to buy the cat a large piece of fresh salmon as a thank you.

The Intelligent Cat

I was having dinner with some people in Northampton once when they suddenly started speaking French to one another. My French is pretty poor but theirs wasn't a good deal better and so I managed to keep up with the conversation. I was just getting into the swing of things when they stopped and went back to speaking English. This happened quite suddenly and apparently without any reason.

'Why did you do that?' I asked Robert, my host.

'Do what?'

'Speak French for a few minutes and then suddenly stop and go back to speaking English.'

'The cat came into the room,' said Robert, as though this explained what had happened. 'But he's gone now,' he added, as though this might be of additional help. I had noticed the cat enter the room but I had not noticed him leave.

I thought about this for a moment, trying to understand. 'Are you telling me that you started speaking French because the cat was in the room?'

'Yes.'

I was still not quite sure that I had understood. 'You started speaking in French when the cat came in?'

'Yes,' said Robert, firmly.

'And you stopped speaking in French when the cat left the room?'

Another nod and an identical answer. 'Yes.' Robert was now beginning to sound rather exasperated.

I thought about this for a little while longer and then slowly shook my head. 'I give up,' I admitted. 'I don't understand.'

'Gilbert is very intelligent,' explained Robert. He lowered his voice and whispered as though worried that someone, presumably Gilbert, might overhear.

'And he understands what you say?'

'We think so,' agreed Robert.

'So, to stop him understanding what you are saying, you speak French when he's in the room?'

'Absolutely right,' agreed Robert.

'But he's very intelligent?'

'Definitely.'

'How do you know he doesn't understand French?' I asked.

'Well, I don't think that's very likely do you?' said Robert. He smiled as he might have smiled at a half-wit. 'After all, he is just a cat.'

'Gilbert is very intelligent,' explained Robert.
He whispered as though worried that someone,
presumably Gilbert, might overhear.

The Proud Father

When I qualified as a doctor we had to take two jobs in hospital before we could work as general practitioners (GPs). In order to be fully 'registered' as medical practitioners we had to survive two six month hospital spells: one working as a house physician and the other as a house surgeon. I took my job as a house surgeon at a hospital in the English Midlands. I shared a house with several other doctors working in the same hospital. The house was an official residence which belonged to the hospital.

Since the house belonged to the hospital there were, as you can imagine very strict rules about what we could or could not do in it. Sleeping and eating were acceptable but most other activities were banned. Keeping pets was definitely pretty high up on the banned list.

Still, we had a huge advantage.

The house in which we lived was separated from the hospital by an extremely busy main road. The downside of this was that when we were off duty but on call we would have to dodge the heavy and unrelenting traffic in order to cross the road. It was a miracle that none of us ended up in the hospital morgue. But the upside was that the administrators and bureaucrats who might have been keen to enforce the regulations had offices in the hospital — on the other side of the same busy main road.

So we had a cat called Hughie living with us.

No one knew just how old Hughie was. Doctors living in the hospital rarely stayed at the hospital for more than one or two six month contracts and so the house had a steady turnover of human occupants. Hughie was the only permanent resident. The generally agreed consensus was that he was somewhere between ten and twenty years of age. We knew he had to be at least ten years old because one of the senior surgical registrars remembered Hughie being there when he'd lived in the house ten years earlier.

However old he was, Hughie was still alert and lively and he spent his nights wandering around the neighbourhood doing all the things tomcats do when they're out on the razzle. We might have been uncertain about his age but we were sure of one thing: Hughie had never been subjected to the veterinary surgeon's knife.

I can say this with some certainty because

of something that happened while I was living there.

I was sitting in the doctors' lounge one Saturday evening, playing chess with an Australian anaesthetist called Arthur, when Hughie suddenly appeared. He was not alone. He was carrying two tiny kittens in his mouth and behind him came a tiny, but very pretty, black and white cat who was carrying another two kittens.

Hughie and the other cat dropped their kittens on the carpet and then Hughie let out a loud miaow, just in case we hadn't noticed what was going on.

Arthur and I turned our attention away from the chess board. One thing was crystal clear and quite indisputable: the kittens were Hughie's.

'Seems like old Hughie's been a busy little fellow,' drawled Arthur admiringly.

'Congratulations!' I said, stroking the obviously proud father.

Arthur and I made quite a fuss of Hughie and his lady. The two cats stayed with us for half an hour or so, allowing us to admire the four kittens. Throughout it all Hughie sat and purred. I'd never seen such an obvious display of pride. And then, without warning, Hughie picked up two of the kittens and headed for the door. The queen picked up the

70

other two and followed him.

'Was that just Hughie showing off?' asked Arthur.

'It seemed like it,' I agreed. 'Let's see where they came from.' I got up from my chair and followed the short procession. With Hughie leading, the two cats headed out onto the pavement and turned left. They walked for about two hundred yards and then turned into an alleyway leading between two terraced houses. I didn't follow but watched them head down towards the gardens behind the houses. It was quite clear that Arthur had been perfectly right. Hughie had brought us his new kittens to admire.

The next day I spoke to one of the Senior House Officers who had lived in the house for a while a couple of years earlier.

'Oh Hughie's still at it, is he?' said the Senior House Officer with a smile. 'When I was living there he brought three families of kittens for us to admire.' He paused, remembering. 'Three different mothers too.'

Hughie didn't bring any more kittens to the house while I was living there but five years later I met a young doctor who'd just finished a job as a junior doctor at that hospital.

'Was there a cat called Hughie still living there?' I asked.

Hughie and the other cat dropped their kittens on the carpet and then Hughie let out a loud miaow, just in case we hadn't noticed what was going on.

'Oh yes!' he replied.

And he told me that while he'd been there Hughie had twice appeared with kittens in his mouth. And on each occasion he had been accompanied by the kittens' mother.

I don't suppose anyone except Hughie has any idea how many kittens he has fathered. But it's probably a good thing he doesn't have to pay kitten maintenance.

The Cat Who Liked To Sleep In

I lived for a while in a house in the English Midlands. I was working as a locum GP and the senior partner at the practice had arranged my accommodation. I couldn't stay in a flat (which I would have much preferred) because my contract required me to be on call for two nights a week and on alternative weekends. I needed to have someone available to take calls for me when I was out visiting patients. My landlady had agreed to take on this added responsibility for an extra fee. (I had a vague suspicion that my land-lady, a stout, elderly woman with very fixed views on an astonishing variety of subjects, was earning more money than I was from the practice.)

The best aspect of my sojourn with this lady was, without a doubt, the fact that she had a cat; an elderly, rather lazy grey-haired cat called Smokey with whom I swiftly established a very warm relationship.

Theoretically, Smokey was expected to spend his nights in his basket in the kitchen. But Smokey wasn't particularly keen on rules and on my first night I awoke at about three in the morning to find him sleeping on my bed. I was awakened by his twitching tail brushing across my cheek. He seemed to enjoy sharing my bed and whenever I woke in the morning I would find him fast asleep and tucked up very close to me.

Since my responsibilities included doing a morning surgery, which started every morning promptly at nine, I had purchased an alarm clock so that I could wake up in plenty of time. My landlady would, I have no doubt, been willing to continue to wake me but I preferred to retain as much independence as I could. On the first two mornings, before I'd acquired my alarm clock, she had woken me by bursting into my bedroom shouting my name and then shaking me by the shoulder. It had been an 'alarming' experience which I was not keen to repeat.

It was on the fourth day after I had bought my alarm clock that my problem started. The alarm, which had worked perfectly for the first three days, didn't go off and, as a result, I didn't wake up when I had expected. I was eventually awakened at fifteen minutes past eight by my landlady.

'Are you getting up this morning?' she shouted, as I reluctantly lurched from dreamland into reality. I rubbed my shoulder. She had big hands and a strong grip. She told me the time and then told Smokey he should be downstairs.

'I thought you'd bought yourself an alarm clock?' she said as the cat stretched, jumped down off the bed and disappeared.

'I did buy a clock,' I said. I picked the clock up from the bedside table and blearily examined it. The clock had a button on the top of its casing. When the alarm was switched on the button was up. To switch off the alarm the button simply had to be pushed down. When I examined it, the button was down. This puzzled me. I felt sure that I'd turned on the alarm when I'd gone to bed. I scrambled out of bed, got dressed and went to work without having time to eat any breakfast. I am not a person who feels comfortable about starting the day without breakfast.

Exactly the same thing happened the next day.

I tested the alarm clock. It worked perfectly well.

When the clock failed to go off for the third morning in a succession I decided that something 'funny' was going on. My first thought, I regret to say, was that someone was turning off the alarm clock after I'd gone to bed. The only possible suspect was my landlady. Why would she do such a thing? I had no idea. But she was a woman who enjoyed her responsibilities. Maybe she felt aggrieved that she had been replaced by an alarm clock.

I decided that in order to find out what was going on I would pretend to go to sleep but would, instead, stay awake and keep watch on the clock. I left the bedroom curtains slightly ajar so that the moonlight filtering into the room would enable me to keep an eye on the clock.

I didn't have long to wait. The clock was turned off about ten minutes after I turned out the light and pretended to go to sleep.

It wasn't my landlady pressing the button down on the top of the alarm clock. It was Smokey.

I watched in astonishment as he crept up the bed until he could reach the bedside table, and pressed down the button on the top of the alarm clock.

It wasn't difficult to understand why.

Smokey loved sleeping and he liked sleeping on my bed. The alarm clock, by removing me from the bed, was disturbing his sleep and interfering with his comfort. And so Smokey must have watched to see how the clock was controlled, and decided to take action accordingly.

I watched, with a smile, as Smokey crept

'Are you getting up this morning?' she shouted.

back down the bed, turned round three times, and went back to sleep tucked up against my thigh. I liked feeling him there but I had to get up in time for the morning surgery and so I got out of bed, picked up the alarm clock, and reset it. I then looked around for somewhere to put the clock where Smokey would not be able to turn it off.

I thought about putting it on top of the wardrobe. But there was, I thought, a very good chance that Smokey would be able to get up there. In the end I opened a drawer in the bedside cabinet, put the primed alarm clock inside, and then almost but not quite re-closed the drawer.

I couldn't help staying awake for a while to watch what Smokey would do.

He must have seen where I'd put the clock because he went straight to the drawer. He tried to open it. But he couldn't. Eventually, in clear disgust, he gave up and went back to sleep beside my thigh.

I felt quite guilty about it.

But I needed my breakfast before I went to work and I really didn't want to be shaken awake by my landlady any more. Smokey must have forgiven me because he slept on my bed for the remainder of my stay in the town.

Three Legs, One Eye And A Third Of A Tail

I once knew a cat who had three legs, one eye and one third of a tail. He was an extremely happy cat who genuinely seemed to enjoy life.

I saw the accident which caused his injuries.

I was on my way to visit a patient when a battered Ford swept past me, travelling on the wrong side of the road. It was going at well above the speed limit. Suddenly, the driver braked. But it was too late. The cat which had leapt out into the road was unable to get out of the way and the car was unable to stop.

When I reached the cat I thought it was dead or dying. I picked it up very carefully, trying to move it as little as I could, wrapped it in a rug and took it to a nearby vet whom I knew quite well.

It wasn't until about two weeks later that I found out that the owners of the cat were patients of mine. They were an elderly couple, quite well off, who lived in a smart, detached bungalow. They had been devastated by the disappearance of their beloved cat, and had assumed that it had been run over and left to die somewhere. It had never occurred to them that the cat might have run away. The couple, both crippled with arthritis, had spent much of the intervening time walking around the neighbourhood looking for their cat. They'd had 'missing posters' printed and had stuck them to trees, lampposts and in the windows of several local shops. It was a poster on a tree that had caught my eye.

They were shocked when I delivered their cat back to them. Both burst into tears. But they were pleased to see it and I knew they would continue to look after it, even though it was now rather less than three quarters of the cat they had last seen.

He couldn't run or climb, of course, but that didn't matter much because for the first time in his life he showed no interest whatsoever in going outside. He became a 'bungalow cat', content to stay indoors and sit on rugs, beds and laps. He managed to get about quite well, hobbling around on three legs, and could even get up onto a chair or a bed without too much difficulty.

Before the cat had been injured he had never shown much interest in me or, indeed, anyone else. He'd been a rover; coming home only to eat and lick his wounds after a fight or another close escape.

But after the injury he changed. He became quite affectionate. And, to my surprise and delight, he always made a beeline for my lap whenever I visited. Even if he was curled up in front of the fire he would get up, hobble over and climb up onto my knees. He would look up at me, nuzzle against my chest, and then curl up. I always ended up staying longer than I needed to, or intended, because I couldn't bear to put him down.

To this day I'm convinced that he knew that I was the one who had rescued him and taken him to the vet. He was, I felt sure, saying 'thank you' to me for saving his life.

I always ended up staying longer than I needed to, or intended, because I couldn't bear to put him down.

The Pampered Cat And The Stray

Friends of mine had a very pampered cat. She was called Sookie and she ran the household as strictly as a sergeant major could have done. Everything revolved around her requirements and her whims.

And then, one day, a stray cat appeared on my friends' doorstep. The stray was very dirty and extremely bedraggled. It looked as though it hadn't eaten for days.

My friends knew that they would have to at least feed the cat but they were very worried about Sookie's reaction. If she saw them feeding another cat she might go into one of her momentous sulks. They didn't think they could cope with that and so they led the stray cat into their utility room, shut it in and fed it there. The utility room (which contained the washing machine and the spin drier) was the only room in the house which Sookie never entered.

The cat was ravenous. It ate two tins of Sookie's very best cat food and two large bowls of milk.

But it would not let them clean its dirty fur. It would not let them touch it at all.

They found an old litter tray of Sookie's, and a basket she no longer used, and put both into the utility room so that the stray cat could stay in some comfort. But they still didn't know what to do for the long term. They were frightened of Sookie's reaction.

And then, two days later, the door which shut the utility room off from the rest of the house was left open and the two cats, smelling or sensing each other's presence, met in the kitchen.

Both my friends happened to be there when the meeting took place.

Neither could quite believe what they saw.

Sookie approached the stray and, without pausing or hesitating, proceeded to clean the stray's fur with her tongue. And the stray, previously so nervous that it seemed almost feral, happily allowed Sookie to do this.

Once the stray was clean, Sookie led it to her own dishes and sat back, allowing the stranger to feed from her own bowls.

When the bowls were empty Sookie walked over to where my friends were standing and miaowed loudly. It was clear that she wanted the bowls refilling. My friends did as they had been instructed.

This time both cats ate together.

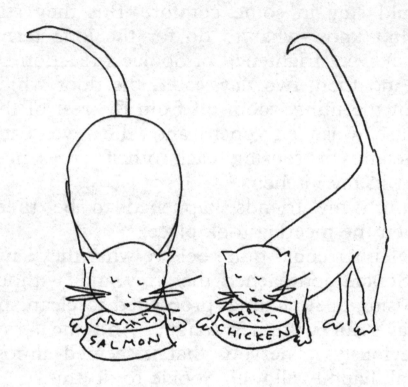

This time both cats ate together.

Now the two cats live happily together.

'It was quite an eye opener for us,' said my friends. 'We had expected Sookie to behave in exactly the opposite way. It seems that we really didn't know Sookie at all.'

The Swiss Cat

I lived once in a Swiss town called Schaffhausen. One of my reasons for going there was to learn to speak German. Sadly, I hadn't realised that in Northern Switzerland the variety of German they speak bears as much resemblance to 'hoch' German or 'proper' German as cockney does to English.

While living in Switzerland I stayed in lodgings with a stern Swiss couple who regarded neatness and punctuality as the only two virtues worth bothering about. Their home was cleaner and tidier than the operating theatres in most British hospitals. The words 'prim and proper' could have been invented for my landlord and landlady. Their idea of wild fun was to go for a walk around the Rhinefall on a Sunday afternoon. Their sole concession to recklessness was to share their home with a cat called Ralfie.

Ralfie was a huge Persian and although he was extremely well looked after he was subject to a variety of restrictions. In the living room he was allowed to climb onto just one easy chair, a chair which was covered in a rug so that any loose hairs could easily be taken outside and removed, he was not allowed onto any of the work surfaces in the kitchen and, most important of all, he was not allowed to go upstairs under any circumstances. Ralfie obeyed these rules as though his life depended upon his obedience which, when I think about it carefully, I suppose it did.

My tiny bedroom was on the top floor of the three storey house and my tiny dormer window overlooked the back garden. I had a bed, a small table, a chair and a thin wardrobe which didn't shut properly unless I used a piece of folded paper to jam the doors. I had use of the bathroom between 7.30 a.m. and 7.50 a.m. and 10.00 p.m. and 10.30 p.m. and was served breakfast in the dining room at 8.15 a.m. every morning except Sunday when, as a treat, it was served at 8.30 a.m. All my other meals I took out, in restaurants and cafes in the town.

Ralfie and I hit it off right from the start. It was clear that he respected his owners, but there wasn't a great deal of love between them. He knew he could rely on them to provide him with decent meals, and they knew that he wouldn't bring mice into the house and would rush outside if he felt the need to get rid of a furball. At night he slept in a basket in the space underneath the stairs. On sunny days he would sit in the garden. If I didn't have anything to do, or anywhere to go, we would sit together on a wooden bench underneath a huge tree.

But the thing I remember about Ralfie was not his obedience but the one time when he did venture upstairs.

I was asleep in bed one night when I was woken by a scratching at my door. It took me a few moments to realise what it was. I got up, padded to the door in my bare feet and found Ralfie staring up at me.

'What are you doing here?' I asked him in a whisper. 'You'll get into terrible trouble if you get caught.'

Ralfie responded to this by brushing against my legs, turning and starting back down the stairs. Puzzled, I watched him go. He came back up and did the same thing again. On the third attempt I understood. He wanted me to follow him. I put on my shoes, pulled a sports jacket on over my pyjamas and followed him down the stairs. He headed straight for the back door, and exited through the cat flap which led directly from the kitchen to the back garden. I didn't have a key to the back door so I was stymied. After a few moments he came back in again. He was slightly puzzled by my insistence that we go out through the front door but accepted it as eccentric but inevitable.

He led me round the side of the house and down into the garden. I felt a bit of an idiot trudging around in my jacket and pyjama trousers at 3 a.m. (the Swiss take everything very seriously and I was worried that I was probably breaking clothes-wearing rules) but it was dark and it seemed unlikely that anyone would be peeping at that time in the morning.

I felt even more at risk when Ralfie led the way across a low fence into the neighbour's garden. But I followed. He led me into a garden shed.

It was dark inside the shed but as soon as I entered I heard a cat miaowing. And when my eyes became accustomed to the dark I could see that a small grey and white cat had got itself caught up in a roll of barbed wire.

I found a pair of gardening gloves (they were far too small and thinner than I would have liked, but they provided some protection) and managed to free the cat. Amazingly it seemed unhurt. It had lost some fur and had a small scratch on its face but, after a miaow of thanks and licking itself all over, it was able to run off out of the shed and disappear.

I closed the shed door and Ralfie and I made our way back home. I felt very proud of

'What are you doing here?' I asked him in a whisper. 'You'll get into terrible trouble if you get caught.

both of us. I had no idea how he'd found the grey and white cat but it was lucky that he had.

When we got back home Ralfie went back to his bed under the stairs and I, after stroking him and tickling him under his chin, made my way back to my bed in the attic.

Ralfie never came upstairs again. Not once. I was there for another six weeks and Ralfie always obeyed the rules. And he and I never spoke of our night-time adventure. It was a secret we alone shared and which, until now, has been shared with no one else.

The Cat Who Watched Television

When I was in my twenties and thirties I appeared on television two or three times a week. I was a regular on an unending series of identical daytime television shows. I was the resident doctor on a breakfast time programme called TV AM and a constant presence on a wide variety of more or less identical magazine programmes which appeared at lunchtime, during the afternoon or in the early evening. Some I helped present. Some I appeared on as an 'expert'.

Since I was also practising full time as a GP, the logistics of being in the places I was supposed to be were sometimes challenging. My early morning television appearances on TV AM used to involve a drive to the local railway station, a two hour train journey, two hectic taxi rides (with a live twenty minute broadcast crammed in between them), a two hour return train journey and a car drive from the local railway station before arriving back at my surgery in time to conduct a late morning surgery and go round on my home visits. Patients who had watched me on television in a London studio would show no little surprise on seeing me in my surgery or on their doorsteps.

At the time I was living with two cats called Dick and Harry. Both were completely black and were physically indistinguishable from each other. I could only tell them apart by their behaviour. Harry was rather distant and superior. Dick was very friendly.

The cleaner who swept my floors and ironed my shirts always had the television set switched on. Even if she was doing something in another room the television in the living room would be left on. She told me that Dick would usually ignore most of the programmes available but that the moment he heard my voice he would sit in front of the TV set, an enthusiastic and committed viewer. (The only other programme Dick enjoyed was snooker. He used to sit on the top of the television set and try to catch the moving balls before they disappeared into the pockets. He was particularly fond of Alex 'Hurricane' Higgins, whose speed around the table kept him very busy.)

And then, one day, I needed to watch a tape of a pre-recorded programme I'd made. I can't remember why. (I hardly ever watched any of the programmes I'd made.) And Dick was in the room, draped around my neck, when I put the tape into the machine.

I have never in my life seen a cat so obviously confused. Dick leapt down and raced over to the television set. He looked at the television screen and then back at me. He ran back and jumped on my lap. He looked at my face. He jumped down and raced back to the television set. It was clearly all too much for him. He found a spot on the rug in front of the fire, turned round three times, lay down, put his tail over his nose and went to sleep.

He never watched television again.

Not even when Alex Higgins was playing snooker.

He looked at the television screen and then back at me.

The Cat Who Saved A Life

When I first started work as a general practitioner I never went to bed before midnight when I was on call. There were always likely to be more calls in the hour before the end of the day.

The calls at this time of day usually came from one of two groups of patients. First, the patients who had gone through the evening in pain or discomfort. They would often telephone between 11 p.m. and midnight when they realised that their problem wasn't going to go away by itself and they didn't think they could get through the night without help. Second, there would be calls inspired by husbands who had come home from the pub to find their baby crying or coughing. 'Have you called the doctor?' the half-drunken husband would demand. 'It's just a bit of a cold,' the wife would explain. 'Well call the bugger now,' the husband would insist. 'I don't want the kid coughing and spluttering all night. He'll keep me awake!' The wife would hesitate. 'It's nearly midnight,' she would point out. 'And it's really just a bit of a cold.' Too drunk for logic the

98

husband would pick up the telephone and demand an immediate visit.

But, of course, not all calls fell neatly into one of those two categories. The call to Mrs Dimmock certainly didn't. It wasn't Mrs Dimmock herself who made the call. It was her neighbour.

'Mrs Dimmock wants you to go round and see her,' said the caller. She gave me the address and some basic instructions. 'Go round the back and up the stone steps. The light is out so you'll have to watch out. The light is always out. The council won't do anything about it. And watch out for glass on the stairs.'

'Do you know what's wrong with Mrs Dimmock?' I asked.

'She didn't say.'

'You've no idea?'

'No. She just asked me to get you to call. She doesn't have a telephone.'

'Do you know if it's urgent? Does she want me to visit her now or in the morning?'

'Now, of course. She wants you now. Why do you think I'm calling now?'

'Some people ring up at night to arrange a morning visit,' I explained. 'Do you live with Mrs Dimmock?'

'No. I'm a neighbour.'

'How did she get in touch with you?'

'She put a message through my letter box.'

'Do you know when she did this?'

'Some time this evening. It wasn't there when I finished my tea.'

'What does it say?'

'It just says to ask you to call,' said the caller, sounding rather exasperated. 'It gave your name and number. And she'd folded it round some money for the call.' She sighed. 'Are you going to visit or shall I call an ambulance?'

'I'm on my way,' I told her.

★ ★ ★

It took me fifteen minutes to drive to the block of maisonettes where Mrs Dimmock lived and twenty minutes to find her front door.

'Oh, I'm glad you've come doctor,' she said. She was wearing a pink quilted dressing gown and had matching pink curlers in her hair. I didn't know her age but I guessed that the next birthday she celebrated which had a nought at the end would have an eight at the beginning.

'What's the problem?' I asked, following her into a narrow, over-furnished hallway.

She didn't reply but simply led the way down the short hall and into an equally

100

over-furnished living room.

'It's Bertie,' she said. 'I need you to look at Bertie.'

I looked around. There was no one else in the room. 'Who's Bertie?'

'My cat.'

I didn't say anything.

'I only noticed it this evening,' she said. 'He's limping.'

I put my medical bag down on the floor and nodded patiently. This was beginning to sound like the sort of night call doctors use to entertain one another at British Medical Association dinners.

'I think he needs his claws trimming.'

'Ah.'

'It's been a while.'

'Who normally clips them?'

'The vet.'

'Wouldn't the vet be the best person to do them this time?'

'Oh I couldn't call the vet,' said Mrs Dimmock. 'It's Sunday evening.'

We both looked at the clock.

'Actually, it's Monday morning,' I corrected her.

'There you are,' said Mrs Dimmock. 'I couldn't call the vet at this time of the night. Not just to trim Bertie's claws.'

'No,' I agreed. 'I suppose not.'

'I think he needs his claws trimming.'

I had never clipped a cat's claws before. But I managed. I used Mrs Dimmock's second best nail clippers.

'You won't make him bleed, will you?' said Mrs Dimmock.

'No,' I promised. 'I won't.' And I didn't.

★   ★   ★

The story doesn't end there.

Two days later I had been visiting another patient in the neighbourhood when I got outside to find an elderly woman with swollen ankles waiting by my car.

'Can I borrow you, doctor?' she said.

'What's the problem?'

'You visited Mrs Dimmock on Sunday.'

I nodded.

'You did her cat's claws.'

'I did.'

'Sooty's claws need trimming,' said the woman.

'Sooty?'

'My sister's cat. Mrs Onions.'

'I'm a doctor,' I reminded her. 'I usually treat people. You really need a vet for a cat.'

'She can't afford the vet,' said the woman.

'Is Mrs Onions a patient of mine?'

'No. She's with Dr X,' said the woman, naming another local general practitioner.

'But Dr X is always very busy.'

I didn't say anything.

'So will you help?'

I followed the woman with the fat ankles into a ground floor flat about two hundred yards away. It took us nearly ten minutes to get there.

'I brought the doctor,' said the woman with the ankles, introducing me to her sister, a skinny woman in her sixties. 'He's come to see to the cat.' I stared at Mrs Onions in horror. She had an early rodent ulcer on her face.

'I'm not making a habit of this,' I told them both when I'd clipped the cat's claws. 'And don't tell anyone I was here cutting his claws.'

They promised they wouldn't, though I didn't believe them for a moment.

'Have you seen anyone about that ulcer?' I asked Mrs Onions. She looked at me as though surprised I'd noticed, though the ulcer was nearly half an inch in diameter.

'I'm a doctor,' I explained. 'We're trained to notice these things.'

'Yes, I suppose so,' she said.

'Have you mentioned it to Dr X?'

She shook her head. 'I didn't like to bother him.'

I opened my black bag and took out some notepaper. I scribbled a note to Dr X, put it into an envelope, licked the envelope, sealed it and handed it to Mrs Onions. 'Go and see Dr X this evening,' I told her. 'And give him this.'

*   *   *

I saw Dr X two weeks later at a post-graduate medical meeting at the local hospital.

'Thanks for sending along Mrs Onions,' he said. 'I got her an appointment at the hospital. Just about got her in time. Another couple of weeks and it would have been too late.'

'Good,' I said. 'I'm pleased.'

'How on earth did you come to see her?' he asked. 'She hardly ever leaves home. Lives with her sister.'

'I was in the neighbourhood and they asked me to pop in,' I explained. As I said it I knew I should have said something else. Anything. Saw her on a bus. Bumped into her in the public library.

Dr X looked at me over his half moon spectacles. 'Really?' he said. 'You can get into trouble for patient poaching,' he told me sternly.

'They wanted me to see the cat,' I explained.

Dr X's mood lightened noticeably. 'Oh,

really? And what was wrong with the cat?'

'It needed its claws trimming,' I muttered. I knew I had gone red.

Slowly, he raised a quizzical eyebrow. 'Oh?' he said. 'I didn't know your practice included cats. Do you do other animals too? Dogs? Parrots? Rabbits? Goldfish?'

'No,' I mumbled. 'Just cats.'

'Ah,' he nodded, smirking. 'A bit of a specialist eh?'

I muttered something unintelligible and hurried off.

But if I hadn't been to clip the cat's claws would anyone have seen Mrs Onions's rodent ulcer in time? I suspect not.

It's no exaggeration to say that her cat saved her life.

The Cat Who Stole Bras

For a while I worked in a medical practice where one of the senior partners held the position of local police surgeon. This meant that when I was on call for the practice I was the official 'stand-in' as police surgeon.

Most of the time the duties involved taking blood from drivers who had failed the breathalyser test. Occasionally, I had to attend murder cases and examine the body. If the police managed to catch a suspect I had to take hair, fingernail and blood samples.

It was while working as the stand-in police surgeon that I managed to help prove the innocence of an unlucky man who had been arrested for stealing underwear from one of his neighbours. It was one of the strangest cases that ever came my way though until now it has never been written about anywhere. The man had a close relationship with the proprietor of the local newspaper and he succeeded in keeping the incident out of the press completely. The man, whose identity I do not intend to reveal, was a respected member of the community. He had a well-paid job, a wife and two teenage children. Publicity would have ruined him whatever the outcome.

I first became aware of the case when I was asked to examine the man after he had been charged with the offence of stealing five brassieres. It might sound a rather comical charge but neither the police nor the accused considered it to be so. I talked to the man for some time and could find no evidence of any mental condition which might explain the peculiar theft with which he was charged. Throughout our interview the man stead-fastly maintained his innocence. I have rarely ever seen anyone under more stress. Towards the end of our conversation, when it became clear to him that I was inclined to believe his claim that he had nothing to do with the theft, he broke down and cried. In his favour was the fact that although they had searched his home and car the police had found no trace of the missing items of underwear. There was no evidence against him — just the fact that the owner of the underwear had seen the man in his own garden several times prior to the disappearance.

As it happened, the woman whose bras had been stolen, was also a patient of mine and so I found myself dealing with both sides of this most unusual case. At her request, I visited her two days after the alleged theft had taken place. I asked her to show me the site of the theft.

Excited by her position as the centre of so much attention the woman happily took me outside and showed me her washing line. She also showed me where the bras had been pegged out prior to their disappearance.

'So they were all at this end of the line?' I said.

She nodded. 'The line runs close to my shed just here. If I peg out anything longer it brushes against the roof when it blows in the wind.'

'So you just put bras here?'

'And other undies, and face flannels and small towels. That sort of thing.'

I don't know why I thought of this but I asked if I might take a look inside the shed. The woman looked at me as though she knew I was wasting my time but said she didn't mind.

We found the bras almost immediately. They had been made into a soft bed in a corner of the shed. There were several other items of lingerie there, together with several odd socks, a couple of face flannels and two teatowels. The woman was very embarrassed at the discovery.

'Do you think they could have been taken by a bird?' she asked. 'A crow?' It was obvious that the washing hadn't been stolen by human hands.

I shook my head. 'Do you have a cat?' I asked, on a hunch.

She said she had.

'Have you any washing you could put out now?' I asked.

She said she had a load in the washing machine waiting to be put out on the line and agreed to peg it out straight away.

We then hid behind a large oak tree in her garden and waited to see what happened.

Within twenty minutes we had the answer.

Her cat, a plump little creature with a black coat and white paws, used a metal table to get up onto the shed roof. From there she could easily reach the nearest items of washing — in this instance a variety of socks, flannels and underwear.

We watched in astonishment as the cat pulled down a sock, bit at the peg to release it, and then carried the sock, in her mouth, down into the shed below. The cat repeated this journey three times.

'You always hang your bras just there?' I asked her.

She said she did and admitted that this was not just so that they didn't catch on the shed roof but also through a sense of modesty, mixed in with a little embarrassment. She was

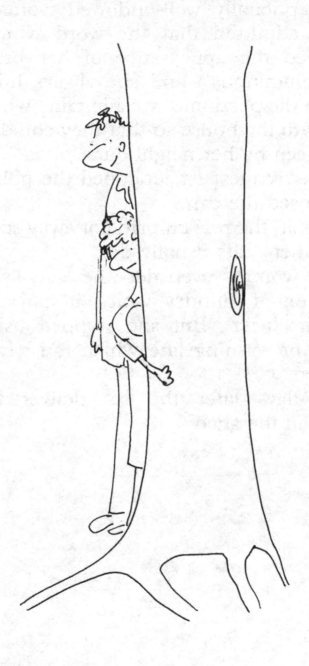

We then hid behind a large tree in her garden
and waited to see what happened.

an exceptionally well-endowed woman (she herself admitted that the word which best described the appearance of her brassieres was 'voluminous') and she always hung her bras on the portion of washing line which was nearest to the house so that they could not be easily seen by her neighbours.

At her request I telephoned the police and they closed the case.

The cat, the real culprit, got away scot-free.

But then, cats usually do.

The woman even let the cat keep the collection of laundry which it had used to make its 'nest'. But she stopped using the stretch of washing line which ran nearest to the shed.

Ten days later the cat delivered three kittens in the shed.

The Cat Who Liked Hiking

A few years ago I was staying for a while with a friend at his house in the country. Naturally, my solitary feline companion at the time, Thomasina, had accompanied me on my visit. The house was quite large and sat in the middle of about twenty acres of pastureland and woodland. Thomasina and I shared a massive old four poster bed in a huge bedroom. It was the first time in my life that I'd enjoyed the delights of a bedroom which was heated by a log fire. Thomasina used to sleep in front of the fire until the final embers had died away and then she'd jump up onto the bed, which was covered with a huge and heavy rug, and curl up next to me.

Every morning, before breakfast, I used to go for a walk around the perimeter of the twenty acres. There was no formal path but the walk took me through a small wood, past a pond and around the edge of several large fields.

Naturally, Thomasina used to accompany me down the stairs when I got ready to go out on one of my early morning walks. To begin with she would sit on the gate leading into the first field and wait for my return, but, after a day or two of this, she started to walk with me. On the first occasion she walked perhaps a hundred yards before turning round and racing back to the safety of the gate. On the second occasion she managed a hundred and fifty yards. On the fifth day she didn't go back. At home she often went on country walks with me; this was nothing new for her.

After three quarters of a mile or so she got tired and let me know that she wanted to ride the rest of the way. I bent down so that she could leap up onto my back and she settled down wrapped around my neck.

Most days I didn't see anyone at all on my walks. But one day I saw a farmer messing with his tractor. When he saw me he stood up, waved and wandered over for a chat. It was a beautiful, crisp winter's day. There was a layer of frost on the ground.

We talked for a while about the weather and the prospects for the next few days.

'You have a cat around your neck,' the farmer said eventually. He told me this as though I might not otherwise have been aware of it.

I looked down, as though I'd forgotten about Thomasina. 'Yes,' I agreed. 'Keeps me warm. I couldn't find my scarf when I came out of the house.'

'You have a cat around your neck,' the
farmer said.

The farmer stared, frowning.

'Cats are quite useful, aren't they?' I said. 'Very adaptable.'

The farmer smiled nervously, in the way people do when they've met someone whom they suspect of being a dangerous lunatic.

Sooty's Miracle

Some patients fight when they are taken ill. They are like the fox who is caught in a trap and who gnaws off his leg in order to escape and survive. Others give up and retreat into themselves. They are like the animal who crawls into a corner, turns his face to the wall, and waits for the inevitable.

Mrs Hodgkinson was like an animal who had crawled into a corner.

She had breast cancer which had been treated successfully with an operation but she was convinced that she was going to die. She went home from hospital, went to bed and prepared for the end.

I tried to tell her that she could be one of the patients who fights cancer and wins. I told her that all she had to do was get her strength back and rediscover her joy for life.

But she wasn't interested. She wouldn't even eat. She lay in bed and lost weight. Her husband, who loved her dearly, was in despair. He did everything he could to persuade her to eat. He made wonderful soups. He liquidised fruits and made exquisite drinks. He had never been a cook but he taught himself how to prepare all sorts of appetising foods. And he put a lot of effort into presenting food so that it looked good.

But nothing worked.

He and I were sitting at her bedside one day, trying, as usual to persuade her to eat. Mr Hodgkinson had prepared a wonderful ice cream and peach concoction. But she wasn't interested. She wasn't thin; she was wasted. She looked like an advertisement for one of those charities that operate in Third World countries where people starve to death.

And then the cat came into the room.

He was on the bed before any of us realised that he had a mouse in his jaws.

He walked up the bed until he was about two feet away from Mrs Hodgkinson. And then he dropped the mouse. It was freshly killed.

We all looked at it, horrified.

If anything seemed guaranteed to put Mrs Hodgkinson off her food the mouse seemed to be it.

'Thank you, Sooty,' said Mrs Hodgkinson. She was so weak that she spoke in a whisper. She smiled.

'Even the cat wants you to eat,' said her husband. There were tears in his eyes.

'Thank you, Sooty,' repeated Mrs Hodgkinson. 'But if you don't mind I think I'd rather

He walked up the bed until he was about two feet away from Mrs Hodgkinson. and then he dropped the mouse.

have the ice cream for now.'

She reached for the dish of ice cream and peaches which was on the bed table in front of her. She picked up the spoon and, slowly, she began to eat.

I reached over, picked the mouse off the counterpane and carried it downstairs. The cat watched me but stayed behind. When I got back upstairs the bowl was half empty.

'Could you eat some soup?' asked Mr Hodgkinson.

'I think I could,' answered his wife.

They were both in tears.

I muttered something about letting myself out and coming back in a day or two.

I didn't want them to see that I was crying too.

Mrs Hodgkinson was up and about a month later. She, her husband and the cat are all still well.

Life Was Never Dull With Alice Around

Alice, the charismatic author of *Alice's Diary* and *Alice's Adventures,* didn't like cat baskets and, over the years, she became extremely skilful at escaping from them. If she'd been prepared to do her escaping to order (rather than simply when she wanted to) she could have had quite a good career as an escapologist. She once bit and clawed her way out of a rather smart looking carrying basket made out of wood and cane, and she utterly destroyed two very stout, specially-made carrying boxes which I had purchased from a well-known national animal charity which had been under the impression that cardboard boxes would be capable of confining cats. Escaping from the wood and cane basket took Alice about thirty minutes of chewing and clawing but the cardboard ones were much easier. I doubt if she was in the second box for more than five minutes before her head poked through the hole she'd made with her claws and teeth.

Alice, like all wilful young ladies, could be

very determined when she didn't want to do something (or when she didn't want to be somewhere) and I gradually learned that it was foolish to try to impose my will on hers. When a prima donna doesn't want to do something (or be somewhere) it makes sound sense (and for a much easier life) if you adapt your expectations to fit her requirements.

And so, whenever it was necessary to take her anywhere, I eschewed boxes and carrying baskets and transported her 'freestyle'. In practice this meant either allowing her to trot along behind, alongside or ahead of me or, if she was tired or wanted a better view of her surroundings, allowing her to ride on my shoulders, with her front paws on one side of my neck and her back paws and tail on the other.

If I thought it likely that she might be startled, run off and be in danger I would attach a collar and lead to her. She could, of course, escape from the collar quite easily if she wanted to but it nevertheless gave me a genuine sense of security. Having proved that she could escape from the collar if she wanted to she was quite happy to keep it on. We both knew it was an optional extra and that she was only wearing it because she was doing me a favour.

I didn't bother with the collar and lead

when she was travelling in the car, of course.

Alice liked travelling by car. It amused and intrigued her. If it was an estate car she would start all journeys standing up at the back of the car with her front paws and nose pressed against the rear window. She would watch the cars behind with great interest and, I am sure, enjoy the interest her presence would inevitably provoke. If we were reduced to travelling in a saloon car (by no means as popular with her as an estate car) she would climb up onto the back parcel shelf and curl up there for a while.

Since she had a short attention span, and rarely stayed in the same position for long, she wouldn't stay in the back of the car for more than ten or fifteen minutes. She would, without notice of any kind, suddenly leap onto my shoulders and sit there for a few moments before deciding what to do next.

Her favourite position was on the area just beneath the windscreen, the stretch of plastic where drivers and passengers usually toss their sunglasses, maps, and bits of papers containing scrawled notes about how to get from Birmingham to Wolverhampton without going via Norwich, but this wasn't something of which I approved. She liked to sit there, right in front of me, staring out of the window and watching the road ahead.

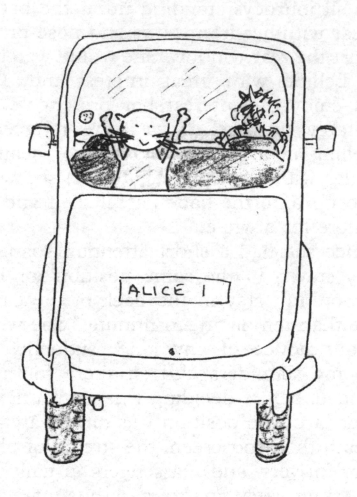

She would start all journeys standing up at the back of the car with her front paws and nose pressed against the rear window.

Naturally, this rather limited my vision and I was reduced to peering around her in order to try to see what was happening up ahead. I used to be quite firm about this and repeatedly move her to one side so that I too could take a look at the road and the traffic ahead. Naturally, she didn't like that. After being moved a couple of times she would get the message and move onto my lap where she would stand with her front paws on the steering wheel and her head peering through or over the spokes. She liked this position a lot. It meant she could treadle my thighs with her rear paws while keeping an eye on the outside world through the windscreen. I always thought this was a pretty safe driving position for us both since, being quite tall, I could see over her head quite well.

But not all motorists shared my feeling.

And one day some busybody with nothing better to do telephoned the police to report that they'd seen a man with a cat on his lap driving a motor car.

I only found this out, of course, after the police car had stopped me.

'Excuse me, sir,' said the policeman, stooping and peering past me into the car. 'But we've had a report that a cat has been helping you drive this motor vehicle.' His patrol car was parked in front of mine. The flashing blue light was still flashing. His colleague was in the front passenger seat, presumably checking me out on their computer. You can, incidentally, tell how long ago this happened by the polite manner in which he addressed me. The 'sir' rather dates the conversation.

'A cat?' I said. 'Helping to drive the car?'

'Sounds strange, I know,' said the policeman. 'But we had a report and we have to check these things out.'

I opened the door and got out of the car. 'Take a look,' I invited.

He leant into the car and looked around. 'There doesn't seem to be a cat in here.' He peered into the back of the car and then checked the passenger footwell. 'Do you mind if I look in the boot?'

I opened the boot lid. He looked inside. A tartan rug, a pair of Wellington boots, half a can of anti-freeze and the usual collection of rags, tissues, cassette tapes, woolly hats, gloves and socks with which the boot of any car I have ever owned has always been festooned within weeks. I never know where the socks come from but they are always there. Maybe they are the socks which disappear from the washing machine.

'Sorry to have bothered you, sir,' said the policeman, closing the boot lid with a slam.

'Bit of a false alarm.' He checked his notebook. 'We'll be having a word with the person who made the allegation. Maybe warn him about wasting police time.'

'Quite right,' I nodded. 'I'm sure you've got better things to do. Burglars to catch and so on.'

'Absolutely, sir,' nodded the policeman. He put his notebook away and refastened his tunic pocket. 'My apologies again for the inconvenience.'

'Don't worry about it, officer,' I said generously. He waved. I waved. He got back into his car. I got back into mine. He drove off. I fastened my seat belt and waited a moment.

'Alice,' I said softly. 'Where are you?'

Nothing. Not a sound.

Alice doesn't like surprises or strangers. Being stopped by a police car with a flashing light on the roof had surprised her. She instinctively knew that the car contained strangers. The moment I'd stopped she'd leapt off my lap. I had no idea where she'd gone. But cats are very good at hiding and I'd never known one more skilful at it than Alice.

'Alice?' I said again. 'Where on earth are you?'

Silence.

'It's safe to come out,' I said softly.

127

There was a miaow. I couldn't tell where it came from.

'Alice?'

Suddenly I felt something soft rubbing against my ankle. I looked down. Alice's head was peeping out from underneath my seat and she was looking up at me. Somehow Alice had managed to squeeze into a space that didn't seem large enough to contain a mouse, let alone a cat.

'Come out!' I said, looking down and laughing.

Alice emerged, shook herself, climbed up onto my lap and rubbed her head against my chest. I tickled her under her chin and stroked her a few times. She purred and assumed her customary driving position and we drove home together.

Life was never dull with Alice around.

Quirky

Jack and Lindsey, a married couple I know, swear that it was their cat who saved their marriage when it went through a bad patch.

He is a dentist and early in his career was working hard to build up a new practice. She had given up her career as a physiotherapist to look after Nicky and Anne, their two small children.

'We just didn't talk much,' confesses Lindsey now. 'Jack would come home shattered and would slump in front of the television with a glass of whisky. Having been at home all day I was desperate for conversation and would sit there fuming. If I tried to tell him about my day — the broken vacuum cleaner, problems with the children, the row at the supermarket check-out — he would just grunt and sip at his whisky.'

'Eventually, we started to row. In order to get his attention I would shout at him. I would wait until the children were in bed and would usually manage to avoid waking them — but I shouted and raved at him like a mad woman. I accused of him of caring for his patients and his practice more than he cared for us — which was terribly unfair of course because he was only building the practice so that he could look after us — and he would snarl back and accuse me of being shrewish and a nag — which was equally unfair because I just wanted him to talk to me and to not shut me out.'

'The problem was that although I didn't wake the children, Quirky, the cat, clearly became upset by our arguments. Quirky was (and still is) a black, short haired cat with a little white bib under his chin. We'd acquired him two years earlier from one of Jack's patients and he had a lovely personality.'

'As soon as I started shouting, Quirky would rush around the room crying and complaining and generally making it pretty clear that he didn't like what was happening. He would rush from one of us to the other and the message was clear: he wanted us to stop rowing and to be friends. He only ever behaved like this when we were having an argument.'

'Things came to a head one day when we were having a particularly ferocious argument. Quirky leapt on top of the television set, knocking off and breaking a hideous vase that my Aunt Jane had bought us, and sat there miaowing at the top of his voice.'

'Suddenly, I started to giggle. And then

Quirky leapt on top of the television set,
knocking off and breaking a hideous vase that
my Aunt Jane had bought us.

Jack started to laugh.'

'I don't think Quirky likes us rowing,' said Jack.

'I said I didn't much like it either. Jack said he wondered if the cat would shut up if he gave me a cuddle. So he gave me a cuddle and Quirky stopped miaowing. He even started to purr.'

'After that we started to talk about things and they were never bad again. I hate to think how bad things might have got if Quirky hadn't intervened.'

My Strangest Ever Prescription

Miss Cuthbertson, a slim, usually elegant woman in her forties, shuffled into my surgery in the village of Bilbury as though she carried all the worries of the world on her shoulders. She looked down at heel and haggard. The last time I'd seen her she'd visited me to have some stitches removed from a small cut in her leg. I looked at her medical records. That had been slightly less than nine months ago. She worked as an assistant manager in a store in nearby Barnstaple.

'I need a tonic,' she said, collapsing into the patients' chair. She had a ladder running up the front of her left stocking. Her hair hadn't been brushed. Her make up looked as if she'd put it on in the dark.

'You look tired,' I said.

'I've not been sleeping very well,' explained Miss Cuthbertson.

'Do you know why?' I asked.

'Oh yes,' she replied. 'I've got a cat.' For the first time since she'd arrived in the surgery she managed a smile. 'She's lovely,' she said. 'A tortoiseshell. Very loving. They are, you know? A friend of mine who knows about cats says they're the most loving type of cat.'

I nodded but I didn't say anything. I knew she'd explain.

'The cat won't go out when I go to bed. She likes to sleep on my bed.'

I nodded, to encourage her.

'But she likes to go out at night.'

'Ah.'

'I'm a heavy sleeper but she's discovered the test button on the smoke alarm.'

'I see. I should imagine that wakes you up.'

'It does.'

'Can't you just move the smoke alarm? Put it out of reach?'

'I don't like to do that,' said Miss Cuthbertson. 'If Trixie wants to go out then it's not right to keep her in.'

'Does she have a litter tray?'

Miss Cuthbertson shook her head. 'Oh no,' she said. 'I tried her with one but she didn't like it.' She paused, thinking about it. 'I even bought her one with a roof over it,' she said. 'In case she was shy.'

'No good?'

Miss Cuthbertson shook her head again.

'Perhaps if you could just give me a tonic?' suggested Miss Cuthbertson. 'I might be able to cope a bit better. I need my sleep, you see.'

Thumper fitted the cat flap that afternoon.
And Trixie and Miss Cuthbertson were both
delighted with it.

'Hmm.' I sounded as unconvinced as I was.

'I don't want a sleeping tablet,' she said. 'Just a tonic will do.'

'You need a carpenter not a tonic,' I told her. 'Why don't you let me get Thumper to pop round?'

'Thumper Robinson?'

I nodded. It is difficult to describe exactly what Thumper Robinson does for a living other than to say that he is a jack of all trades and a master of most. He does odd jobs, buys and sells cars and deals in antiques.

'What can Thumper do?' asked Miss Cuthbertson, looking sceptical.

'Fix a cat flap in your back door,' I told her. 'Then Trixie will be able to go in and out whenever she wants and you'll be able to sleep through the night.'

'What a wonderful idea!' said Miss Cuthbertson. Some people might have looked embarrassed at not having thought of it. She didn't. She just looked pleased.

Thumper fitted the cat flap that afternoon. And Trixie and Miss Cuthbertson were both delighted with it.

Kipper

I once had a patient who had the same medical condition as her cat. Even though I was not, of course, treating the cat, I can confirm that the cat was the much better patient of the two.

Mrs Tipford was a retired actress. She had appeared in repertory theatre in Glasgow and Plymouth and all theatres between. She had even appeared once or twice on television — usually as a walk on role in one of the weekly soap operas. She had once played a piece of melon in a television advertisement. Her flat was festooned with photographs of famous people she'd met and had herself photographed with. On her mantelpiece alone there were photographs of her with Sir Alec Guinness, Sir Ralph Richardson and Sir John Geilgud. Each photograph was signed by the relevant knight.

Mrs Tipford was a maturity onset diabetic. She was no more than five foot three inches tall and weighed fourteen stones. We both knew that she was diabetic because she ate too much and was grossly overweight.

Kipper, the cat, was adorable and knew it.

She was the sort of cat who becomes devoted to a human being. Everywhere Mrs Tipford went Kipper wanted to be. Everything Mrs Tipford did Kipper wanted to be part of it. Kipper always wanted to be the centre of attention. If Mrs Tipford sat down to read a magazine, Kipper, who up until that moment had shown no interest whatsoever in the magazine, would suddenly decide that she had to sit on it.

She was the sort of diabetic cat who needed injections. But she was, the vet assured me, a perfect patient. She needed injections twice a day and she would come into the house at precisely the right times; sitting patiently while Mrs Tipford gave her the necessary jab.

Mrs Tipford took tablets to try to boost her pancreas into producing more insulin. And she was supposed to be on a strict diet. But, although she managed to take her tablets regularly she was less assiduous about sticking to the diet. If I told her to cut out cream buns she would simply increase her intake of doughnuts. If I told her to half her consumption of hamburgers she would double her consumption of cheeseburgers.

'But I'm doing what you told me, doctor!' she would insist.

The cat stayed well. Mrs Tipford did not.

'You have to think you are playing the part of a thin person,' I told her. 'Eat less. Eat much less. Behave like a thin person. Be a thin person.

Mrs Tipford started to show serious signs that her illness was beginning to affect her body. She developed ulcers on her feet. And I became seriously worried about her.

'If you go on at this rate you'll kill yourself,' I told her one day, deciding that bluntness might work where encouragement and cajoling had failed.

The comment, though apparently cruel, had the desired effect. Mrs Tipford looked shocked. I decided to go for the kill.

'And if you die, who will look after Kipper?' I asked. 'Who will give Kipper her daily injections?'

Mrs Tipford went pale.

'You should think about it,' I told her. 'Without you, how many people would be prepared to look after a diabetic cat?' I paused for a moment to let the thought sink in. 'Someone would probably ask the vet to have her put to sleep.'

'Oh no!' cried Mrs Tipford, horrified.

'It's up to you,' I told her. 'Your diabetes is not that serious. It's controllable. But you have to want to control it.'

'Oh I do want to control it,' said Mrs Tipford quickly. 'Tell me what I have to do. Tell me, please, doctor.' She spoke with an earnestness I'd never seen in her before.

'You have to think you're playing the part

of a thin person,' I told her. 'Eat less. Eat much less. Eat sensibly. Behave like a thin person. Be a thin person.'

And that, to my delight and astonishment, is what Mrs Tipford became.

It took her two months to lose two stones in weight. And another month to lose another half a stone. Her health improved enormously.

Both she and Kipper lived another six years.

And in the end it was Kipper who succumbed first. She was nineteen years old when she went to sleep and didn't wake up.

Mrs Tipford cried a good deal, of course.

'But I made it, didn't I, doctor?' she said. 'I lived long enough to look after her until the end.'

'You did,' I agreed.

'I would have done anything for that cat,' she said.

'I know,' I nodded.

'It was my greatest part you know,' she said. 'Playing the thin person.' She sighed and wiped away a tear. 'But there's no need for me to play the thin person any more,' she said. She thought for a moment or two. 'It was never a role I felt entirely comfortable with.'

Within a month she had put on a stone.

Within three months she had put on two stones.

Within six months she was dead.

Kipper had kept her alive.

And when Kipper died Mrs Tipford simply ate herself to death.

Clever Cats

I have known a number of cats who were capable of operating electrical equipment to their advantage. In the 1980's my cat Alice (the eponymous author of *Alice's Diary* and *Alice's Adventures*) would often turn on my IBM electric typewriter and then curl up against it. The switch that turned on the machine wasn't easy to operate but she did it almost daily for several years until I replaced the machine. I am convinced that two things about the machine appealed to her. First, when it was switched on it made a loud 'purring' sound. Second, within a few minutes it became quite warm. It wasn't difficult to see why she liked the machine and was quite miserable for several days when it broke down and had to be replaced. (As I remember it worked well apart from the fact that it refused to print the letter 'e'. If you've ever tried to type a sentence — let alone a whole book — without using the letter 'e' you will know how troublesome this was. For Alice's sake I persevered for as long as I could but eventually got fed up of writing the letter 'e' into the appropriate place on each page.)

But Alice isn't the only cat to have mastered electrical equipment to her own advantage. A cat called Henry, with whom I once shared a home, proved to be even more adept at manipulating his immediate environment to his advantage.

I'd been living with Henry for about a year and a half when I started waking up at night feeling very hot. At first I thought I was running a temperature but when I realised I wasn't I wandered around the house and found that all the radiators were boiling hot. When I checked with the boiler I found out that it had apparently ignored the thermostat and had turned itself on. The next morning I called the central heating engineer and booked an appointment. 'We're rather busy right now. We can get someone to you in three weeks.'

'But you offer a 24 hour service!'

'Yes, sir, we do.'

'But you just offered to get someone to me in three weeks!'

'We promise to answer your call within 24 hours, not to deal with your problem within 24 hours.'

And then one night the television turned itself on too.

I woke up boiling hot and when I got up to switch off the boiler I could hear the television set talking to itself down in the living room.

I picked up a golf club and tiptoed downstairs. With my heart in my mouth, I threw open the door to the living room. And found Henry sitting watching television.

I picked up a golf club (don't ask what a golf club was doing on the landing — it's a complicated and boring story) and tiptoed downstairs. With my heart in my mouth I threw open the door to the living room.

And found Henry sitting watching the television. (Since you ask it was a cartoon channel.) He looked quite peeved when I switched off the television set and took him to his basket in the kitchen.

The next night I stayed up to find out how he did it.

It was unbelievably simple.

He went into the utility room where the boiler was kept and leapt up onto the washing machine. From there he could easily reach the override button which turned on the boiler. He then padded into the living room, jumped up onto the table on which the television stood and turned on the TV set. He then settled down, in the warmth, to watch TV.

I was so impressed that I was tempted to let him carry on having his 3 a.m. fun.

But I need my sleep and so I'm afraid I got into the habit of pulling out the television plug and locking the door to the utility room.

Not even Henry could put a plug in its socket and unlock a door.

Though I wouldn't bet against eventually coming across a cat who could.

The Pawprint Legacy

I stood up, put my stethoscope into my pocket and took out my prescription pad.

'You've got a rough sounding chest,' I told Mrs Dunberry. 'You'll need an antibiotic. Have you got someone who can take a prescription to the chemist for you?'

She shook her head.

I put the prescription pad away and reached for my black medical bag. 'I'll give you a week's supply,' I told her, rummaging around in my bag and taking out a box of antibiotic capsules. 'I'll get the nurse to call in and see you tomorrow.'

Mrs Dunberry nodded. 'Thank you,' she croaked.

'How on earth did you get like this?' I asked her. 'I haven't seen many chest infections so far this winter.'

'I got soaked coming back from Barnstaple last Thursday,' she whispered.

'Last Thursday?' I remembered it. It had been an awful day. 'It poured down all day,' I said. 'Why on earth did you go out?'

'I had an appointment at the dentist's,' Mrs Dunberry explained.

As I left I couldn't help feeling puzzled. I thought that Mrs Dunberry had a dark blue estate car — I had seen her on many occasions driving one of the old-fashioned ones with real wood on the sides — and couldn't understand why she had caught the bus. The nearest stop for the Bilbury to Barnstaple bus was at least half a mile from her cottage. Before I left I peeped in through the garage windows. The estate car was sitting there, warm and cosy and well protected from the elements.

During dinner that evening I asked my wife why on earth she thought Mrs Dunberry would catch the bus when she had a perfectly good motor car in her garage.

'She doesn't take it out in the rain,' she explained.

I put down my knife and fork and stared at her, disbelievingly.

'Honestly!' she said, quite seriously. 'The car has muddy pawprints all over it and she doesn't want to risk having them washed off.'

'How on earth do you know that?'

'Mrs Pringle told me.'

Mrs Pringle had a smallholding and delivered eggs once a week in her battered and noisy Citroen 2CV. Mrs Pringle knew more about what was going on than anyone in the area. She was an invariably accurate source of gossip. I had heard it said that the editor of the local paper often telephoned her to check on stories before printing them.

'Did Mrs Pringle explain why Mrs Dunberry wouldn't want paw prints washed off her car?'

'Of course. The paw prints are all that there is left of Pippa.'

'Pippa being a cat?'

'Of course. Pippa was a tortoiseshell cat who died about four months ago. She was quite old — eighteen or nineteen I think.'

'No photos?'

'Apparently not.'

'So she protects the pawprints because they're all she's got left?'

'Exactly.'

I picked up my knife and fork and carried on with my dinner. But I couldn't get the story my wife had told me out of my head.

The next morning, after surgery, I drove round to see Mrs Dunberry. I had the best excuse in the world for visiting.

'I feel quite a bit better today, thank you, doctor,' she said. She was sitting in an easy chair in her living room. Most people have their favourite chair facing the fireplace or the television set. Mrs Dunberry had her chair facing the French doors which led out onto her garden. And it was a beautiful garden. I pulled my stethoscope out of my pocket and she pulled aside her dressing gown and unbuttoned her nightdress. I listened to her chest.

'Things sound much better in there,' I told her when I'd finished examining her. I put my stethoscope away. She rebuttoned her nightdress and adjusted her dressing gown.

There was a narrow winding path leading away from the window, and on each side of it grew beds of colourful flowers — exactly the sort of flowers you'd expect to see in a country cottage garden.

'I see all sorts of things from here,' she told me when she'd finished. 'Squirrels, butterflies, birds, rabbits.' She looked up at me. 'I love all animals,' she said.

'You used to have a cat, didn't you?'

'Pippa,' said Mrs Dunberry quietly. 'A lovely tortoiseshell.'

'I love cats,' I told her. 'Beautiful, intriguing animals. When I was a kid I had a cat who went for walks with me. I've been mad about cats ever since. I bet you have all sorts of wonderful memories of Pippa.'

Mrs Dunberry didn't reply at once.

I waited, enjoying the view.

'If I had to go out she would sulk for exactly thirty minutes whenever I came back,' she said.

I smiled and nodded.

'Pippa would watch me come in and then she'd just disappear,' said Mrs Dunberry. 'I never had any idea where she went. She'd race out of the house and I wouldn't see her for thirty minutes.'

'Then she'd come racing back in and demand lots of attention and heaps of love?'

'Exactly!' said Mrs Dunberry. 'How did you know?'

'I had one just like that,' I told her. 'Used to sulk for a whole hour if I'd been away.'

'She would run to me, make a sort of chirruping sound and leap up onto me. She used to sit on my lap and reach up and touch my chin with her paw — with the claws carefully sheathed, of course.'

'Lovely,' I whispered. 'Their paws are like velvet aren't they?'

Mrs Dunberry didn't answer right away. She was too busy remembering.

'She used to sit on the back of my chair and clean my hair,' said Mrs Dunberry. 'As though she was looking for tangles to untangle.' There was a pause. 'Maybe she was looking for insects,' she laughed.

I murmured understanding. 'They break our hearts when they go but they always leave us with such wonderful memories, don't they?'

Mrs Dunberry looked up at me.

'Cats,' I explained. 'They break our hearts

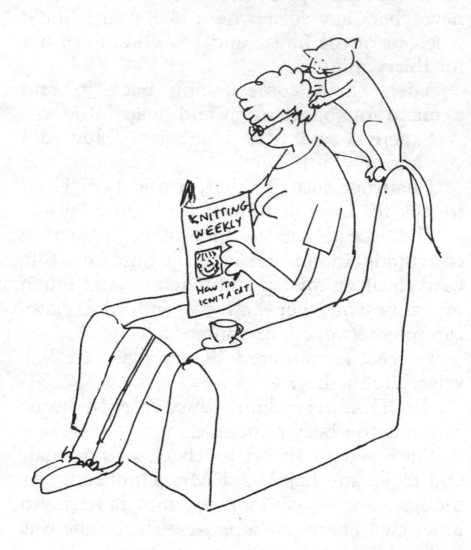

'She used to sit on the back of my chair and clean my hair,' said Mrs Dunberry. 'As though she was looking for tangles to untangle.'

but they leave us with such wonderful memories.'

'Oh they do,' said Mrs Dunberry.

There was a short silence.

'She used to like to play football with a small clay marble,' said Mrs Dunberry. 'It was yellow. It got lost under the sideboard once. She was very upset. I had to get an old curtain rod from the attic and fish it out. I used to flick the ball back to her with my foot and then she'd tap it back to me with her paw.'

'I had one who liked doing that,' I said. 'She'd play for ages with a rolled up ball of silver paper. And then, quite suddenly, she'd decide she'd had enough and she'd go off and have a wash. She usually decided she'd had enough when I managed to hit the ball past her.'

Mrs Dunberry laughed out loud. 'Oh yes!' she said. 'That was just like Pippa. She could be a terrible sulk.'

We both stared out of the window for a while, thinking about cats.

'She hated cold food,' said Mrs Dunberry suddenly. 'If I served her cat food straight out of the tin she would go and sit by the stove to let me know she wanted it warming up.' She looked up at me. 'She wouldn't eat it unless it was warm,' she said.

'Like a mouse,' I said.

She frowned.

'Warm like a mouse,' I said. 'I think that's

why they like warm food.'

'Is it really?' asked Mrs Dunberry. 'I didn't know that.'

We talked for another ten minutes or so about Pippa and about cats in general. She told me about all the little things that Pippa did. She talked about her with great love and with pride too.

'I hadn't really thought about her before today,' said Mrs Dunberry when I told her that I'd better get on with my visits. 'Not properly. Not about the things she did and the way she was.'

'Memories can be very comforting,' I told her.

She nodded. There were tears in her eyes. But they weren't tears of sadness.

'They're the real legacy our friends leave us,' I said.

'I'll never forget her,' said Mrs Dunberry.

'Of course you won't,' I said. 'She was a big part of your life.'

Mrs Dunberry looked up at me. 'Shall I tell you something silly?'

I looked down at her and smiled. 'If you like.'

'I got soaked because I wouldn't use the car. And I wouldn't use the car because I didn't want Pippa's pawprints washing off.'

'That's not silly,' I said. 'I can understand that.'

'Yes, but they were just pawprints,' said Mrs Dunberry. 'I thought they were all I'd got. But they weren't important at all. I've got all these lovely memories.'

I reached down and squeezed her hand.

* * *

Ten days later my wife and I were having breakfast.

'I saw Mrs Dunberry yesterday,' said my wife. 'I was parking the car in Barnstaple. She was putting some parcels into the back of her estate car.'

I smeared home-made marmalade onto a piece of toast.

'She looked very well.'

'Good. I'm pleased to hear it.'

'She must be over that chest infection.'

'She made a pretty quick recovery.'

'But the funny thing is, it was pouring with rain.'

I finished smearing the marmalade, thought for a moment and nodded. 'It rained all day yesterday,' I agreed. 'Bucketed it down.'

'The pawprints had all been washed off her car.'

'Really?'

'And she didn't seem to be in the slightest bit worried about it.'

I nodded. 'Good,' I said. 'Jolly good.' I took a bite of my toast.

The Truce

During one winter a fox regularly visited the house. One morning during a spell of particularly bad weather I spotted him coming out of the big barn where he had been sleeping. There was snow on the ground and the temperature outside was well below freezing. The barn must have made a good shelter from the wind, the snow and the cold.

That afternoon Alice and the fox spotted each other in the courtyard. Tails up, back hair bristling, they circled slowly like a pair of prizefighters assessing each other.

I was worried sick but too nervous to do anything. In fact, I didn't dare move at all. My big fear was that I might distract Alice and give the fox an advantage.

But in the end they didn't fight at all. They simply backed away from each other. Alice was very pleased with herself afterwards.

This happened, to my knowledge, four or five times but the two animals never fought.

Then one day Alice came to me while I was in my study and started to miaow. At first I thought she wanted food so I got up and followed her downstairs. But she didn't go to the area where I kept her bowls and dishes. Instead, she headed for the back door, waited while I put on a pair of shoes, and then led me outside to a hedge at the bottom of the garden.

There, to my astonishment, I found the fox.

He had clearly been injured and was lying, quite still, on a patch of dead bracken. I have no veterinary training but I didn't need any to see that the animal had a broken leg. I had no idea what other injuries he had but it was clear that there were more. I ran back to the house and collected a pair of thick gardening gloves and an old rug. Then, wearing the gloves and using the blanket to wrap him in, I carefully picked up the fox and carried him to the car. Alice followed behind. When I put the fox and the blanket onto the front seat of the car, Alice tried to climb in too. I told her she had to stay at home because we were going to the vet. The word was enough to send her scurrying into the house.

The vet kept the fox for ten days and then rang me and told me that I could pick him up.

'You can release him where you found him,' he said. 'He's still weak but he'll be fine.' I did as I was told.

Two days later I spotted Alice and the fox

I got up and followed her downstairs.

circling each other in the courtyard.

For some reason Alice's compassion towards the fox reminded me of the time during the First World War when, one Christmas Day, British and German soldiers held a temporary truce, during which each side collected its dead and wounded and temporarily stopped fighting one another. When the truce was over the two sides went back to trying to kill one another.

The Cat As Towel

One of the joys of living in a village where everyone knows what everyone else has for breakfast (and finds the information interesting) is also one of the hazards. When you choose to live in Bilbury (or village like it) you have to accept that you sacrifice your privacy. The community becomes your family, and your private business becomes their business.

Many modern villages virtually run into the next village or town and they have little or no real independence. As urban developers spread their housing estates, supermarkets and shopping malls further and further outwards so many once independent small villages are swallowed up and although they may remain alone in name they become, for all practical purposes, merely part of something much larger.

The village of Bilbury, where I live, has no near neighbours. The nearest traffic lights and street lights are a good half an hour's drive away in Barnstaple. The villagers of Bilbury live, survive and thrive alone. We don't have much contact with the outside world and, to be honest, we don't want it. We welcome visitors, of course, and we are comfortable with the fact that a handful of cottages are now owned by 'townies' who visit at weekends and for holidays (though we would take a dim view if they were to bring their food and other supplies with them rather than purchasing their requirements from Peter Marshall's shop), but our attitude to the outside world is simple: you leave us alone and we'll leave you alone.

The result of this isolationist attitude is, of course, that we tend to live in one another's pockets rather more than city dwellers might find entirely comfortable. Our doors are never locked and we all tend to wander into one another's homes without much knocking on doors and with absolutely no telephoning ahead to see if it is 'convenient'.

At the time of which I write, my study, a large, well-lit, airy room with a huge fireplace and a bay window fitted with a window seat, was at the front of the house. The disadvantage of the room's position was that anyone passing by, in the lane which passed the house, could, with just a glance, see whether I was in the room.

If I was visible, sitting at my desk or in an easy chair by the fire, the passer-by would wander over and tap on the window. The vicar would stop by to remind me that I'd promised to run the bottle stall at the local fete and to ask me to make sure that there weren't too many jars of chutney, the president of the Women's Institute would call in to ask if my wife and I would dig out anything suitable for their bring and buy sale, Thumper Robinson would pop in to ask if the kettle still worked, and local antique dealer Patchy Fogg would call in to see if I wanted to accompany him to an auction in Combe Martin, Lynton or South Molton.

However, on the late summer afternoon of which I write I was not in my study but had just clambered out of the bath. I had been working on a new book and had got stuck. One of the things which I have always found helpful in circumstances such as this is a warm bath. And our old-fashioned Victorian claw-footed bath was particularly good for this. It was almost long enough and wide enough to swim in and vastly superior to those modern baths which are too short to allow the bather to stretch out properly.

When I finally hauled myself out of the bath (with the solution to my editorial problem scribbled in pencil in a rather damp notebook) I realised that there was no towel on the rail. There were no spare towels in the bathroom cupboard so, dripping water with every step, I headed downstairs to the airing cupboard in the kitchen. (Don't ask why the airing cupboard is in the kitchen because the answer, though logical is complex and involves a greater understanding of our domestic plumbing and heating arrangements than need concern you. We also have a bread oven in one of the spare bedrooms.)

I had taken barely two steps into the kitchen when I realised that I was not alone. There was an intruder in the pantry, rummaging around among the food stored in there. It was not, I knew, my wife. She was at the Duck and Puddle public house helping Gilly, the landlady, fit new cushion covers on the chairs in the public bar. She was not due back for several hours.

'Who's there?' I demanded, my surprise temporarily forcing me to forget that I was standing there absolutely naked and soaking wet. I took two strides towards the pantry door.

'Oh, there you are, doctor!' called Miss Robinson. 'I didn't want to disturb you. I saw your wife at the Duck and Puddle. She said I could help myself from your pantry for the harvest festival.'

It was only while she was explaining what she was doing that I suddenly remembered that I was naked. The fact that I was dripping

I grabbed the only item I could see —
Thomasina — and clutched her to me, hoping
that she'd keep her claws sheathed.

water all over the kitchen floor no longer seemed of any consequence. I looked around, desperately searching for something — anything — with which to hide my nakedness. A tea towel, a tablecloth, some drying laundry, a newspaper, a discarded coat, a dishcloth — anything.

In the very moment that Miss Robinson emerged from the pantry, clutching an armful of jars, I grabbed the only item I could see — Thomasina — and clutched her to me, hoping that she'd keep her claws sheathed.

'Would you tell your wife that I've taken four jars of her plum jam and four jars of her pickled onions,' said Miss Robinson.

'I've just had a bath,' I explained uneasily. 'Not dry yet.'

'So I can see,' said Miss Robinson. 'I would have thought,' she said, 'that as an animal lover you would have used a towel to dry yourself. Drying yourself on the cat! Really, doctor!'

I tried to explain but she'd gone.

No one in the village ever said anything about it to me and so until now I've never had a chance to explain what happened — and how I appeared to be using a cat as a towel.

The Life Saver

My wife and I were staying in Sidmouth, in South Devon, for a few days holiday. Sidmouth is one of the few places in England which seems to have remained pretty well unchanged over the years.

Every morning, after breakfast, we got into the habit of taking a walk around the town. And each day we ended up sitting on one of those wooden benches kindly donated by relatives and friends commemorating the lives of lost companions. The bench we chose overlooked the sea. Behind us there was a row of Victorian cottages.

Each day, within five minutes of our sitting down on the bench, we were joined by a huge, elderly and distinguished looking marmalade coloured tomcat.

On the first day he just sat between our feet and, like us, stared out to sea.

On the second day he jumped up onto my lap and allowed me to stroke him. When I stopped he turned and looked up at me as if to say: 'What did you stop for? Get on with it!' After a while he would climb onto my wife's lap and allow her to make a fuss of

166

him. He was very fair with his favours.

This exceedingly pleasant routine continued for five days.

On the sixth day the cat, who, with a
shameful lack of originality, we knew as
Ginger, appeared in front of us but wouldn't
jump onto either of our laps. I reached down
and stroked him. He didn't seem interested.
Instead he reached up with one paw and
tapped me on the side of the knee. As he did
this he miaowed.

'I think he wants something,' said my wife.

The cat stopped tapping my knee and
walked away a few paces. He sat and stared at
us. Actually, 'glared' would be a better verb.
He then came back and tapped me on the
knee again.

'He wants us to follow him,' said my wife.

I looked at her. Her interpretation seemed
to make sense. She stood up. Ginger started
to walk away. Every few yards he would stop
and turn back to make sure we were
following.

We followed him back across the road,
down a side street and into a small cul de sac.
The houses there were all small and neat.
Each one had a small, well-tended front
garden. It was summer time and the smell of
the flowers was intoxicating.

Ginger walked through an open gateway

and along a concrete path which ran along the side of one of the houses. We looked at one another, hesitated for a moment and then followed him.

At the end of the path Ginger turned right. We followed him and found ourselves outside the back door of one of the houses. Ginger sat down and miaowed loudly.

'He wants us to go inside,' said my wife.

'Maybe he just wants us to let him into the house,' I suggested.

'There's a flap,' my wife pointed out. And, indeed, there was.

I tried the door knob. The door was locked. Ginger looked up at me and then walked across to where a flower pot containing geraniums stood on two house bricks. He put a paw in between the two bricks and scratched at something. I walked across to him and bent down. Reaching in between the two bricks I found a key.

I picked up the key and stood up.

'It's got to be the key to the back door,' said my wife.

It was.

I opened the back door and called out. 'Is there anyone at home?' Ginger slipped around my legs and entered the kitchen.

There was no answer in response to my call. I tried again. There was still no reply.

'It's got to be the key to the back door,' said
my wife.

'You wait here,' I told my wife. Ginger, already heading for the other door out of the kitchen, turned to check that I was following him.

The solitary occupant of the house was sitting in a chair in the living room. He was pale, sweating and almost unconscious. He was having difficulty breathing and couldn't talk, let alone shout for help. I picked up a wrist. His pulse was thin and thready.

It wasn't difficult to guess that he'd had a heart attack.

An hour or so later he was in hospital. The next door neighbour, a kindly widow who had two cats of her own, kindly agreed to feed Ginger and to keep an eye on him.

I rang the neighbour after we got back home to see how things were. Two weeks after being admitted to hospital the man was back home making a spectacular recovery.

The doctors and nurses who looked after him took the credit for his recovery but it was Ginger who saved his life.

Cats and Telephones

Cats hate being ignored (unless they want to be left alone, of course).

Of all the cats I have known none hated being ignored more than Alice, the mixed tabby who helped me write *Alice's Diary* and *Alice's Adventures*.

When I was working as a GP and had just started writing books I used to spend hours on the telephone. Alice didn't like this at all. When I was on the telephone, talking to someone who wasn't even there, I couldn't possibly provide her with all the attention she deserved.

And so she developed a little trick to end my conversations when she thought they'd gone on long enough.

She would, quite gently, put a paw down on the telephone rest and break the connection. She would do this slowly, deliberately and while looking at me. Her paw would hover above the telephone for a moment, just to let me know what she was planning.

And then, slowly, she would lower it and cut the connection.

She would then climb onto my lap, or my

she would put a paw down on the telephone
rest and break the connection.

shoulders, and take her rightful place at the centre of my attention.

Writing about this reminded me of another cat I knew who used to operate her owner's telephone.

I had a patient called Mrs Bradshaw who was rather deaf. My receptionist came in to see me one day and told me that Mrs Bradshaw had asked me to telephone her.

'You'll have to let the telephone ring for a while,' said my receptionist.

'Can she hear the telephone?' I asked.

My receptionist shook her head. 'Her cat answers the telephone for her,' she explained.

I stared at her, rather disbelievingly.

'Let the phone ring,' she said. 'The phone will be answered but there will be quite a long silence after it seems to have been picked up. Then you will hear Mrs Bradshaw's voice. You have to shout, of course.'

I looked at her and raised a questioning eyebrow.

'When the telephone rings her cat rushes over to it and knocks the phone off the cradle,' she explained. 'She then fetches Mrs Bradshaw to let her know that there is a telephone call for her.'

I telephoned Mrs Bradshaw and things happened exactly as I had been told.

I was so astonished by this that I drove

round to Mrs Bradshaw's home after I'd finished my visits that day. I then telephoned my surgery and asked my receptionist to call me back. When the phone rang I stood and watched in amazement as Mrs Bradshaw's cat did exactly what the receptionist had said she would do.

The End

When my beloved cat Alice was so ill that life was too painful for her to bear, the vet gave me a barbiturate injection to give her. I worried that I wouldn't know when to give the injection but the worry was needless. I knew. Alice came upstairs while I was taking a bath. She sat on the edge of the bath, dribbling blood stained saliva. Gingerly, every movement clearly painful, she stepped onto my chest and sat down. She was so thirsty she tried to drink some of the bath water but she could not. She had a tumour in her mouth which made it impossible for her to eat or drink. (When I'd first reported a speck of blood on her lip and found a tiny lesion inside her cheek the vet had dismissed the finding as of no importance. I still wonder how much longer she might have lived if the vet had been more alert.) Afterwards, I sat her on my lap and tried to inject her with the barbiturate the vet had given me. My hand was shaking and tears were pouring down my cheeks. I fitted the needle and filled the syringe. Then, with Alice sitting on my lap, I said goodbye, stroked her head and tried to give her the fatal injection.

I missed her body completely and felt the needle go through my dressing gown and pyjama trousers and into my thigh. Fortunately, I had the presence of mind not to depress the plunger. I might not have been here to write this if I had.

I rang the vet.

Later I buried her in the garden in a wooden coffin. I put her favourite jumper and copies of her two books in with her. And I paid a local stonemason to prepare a headstone for her grave. 'Get another kitten to replace her,' said well-meaning friends who didn't understand.

Alice died on the 12th May 1992.

I still miss her terribly.

And I know I always will.

'I said goodbye, stroked her head and tried to give her the fatal injection.

The Author

Vernon Coleman has been a confirmed cataholic for as long as he can remember. The first known photograph of him in existence shows him clutching a cat to his chest. He has been resisting treatment for his cataholism for sixty years and consequently, his condition has continued to deteriorate. He is very pleased about this and hopes that it will continue until the end. He likes all cats, of all shapes, sizes and colours, and is particularly delighted when they give some sign that they are prepared to tolerate him.

Vernon Coleman writes: 'Some people make friends when they travel. I have an acquaintance who can't pop into the local supermarket without finding new chums to add to his formidable Christmas card mailing list. If he goes for a walk in a deserted park he will somehow come back with half a dozen new chums. I'm not very good at making friends. Too shy, I suppose. But everywhere I go I meet cats and now, I'm proud to say, I have cat friends everywhere. One of the good things about having cats as friends is that they demand nothing and expect nothing. (Obviously, cats who have become 'family' expect a great deal and demand very much more.) And it's easy to meet new cats. I find that I always seem to find affectionate cats in churches and church-yards. During the last two weeks, for example, I have met and had long, meaningful conver-sations with, cats in churches in Barnstaple, Exmouth, Sidmouth and Wells. Cats may pretend to be indifferent but they often seem to me to be just as keen to make new human acquaintances as I am to make new cat acquaintances. For example, outside a church in Exmouth the other day I saw a black cat rubbing itself against the gate into the churchyard. I bent down to stroke its head and the cat ignored me completely, moving slightly out of reach each time I tried to touch it. Since I was in something of a hurry at the time I stood up and started to move away. The cat immediately stopped rubbing itself against the gate and ran after me. He then stood still while we got to know each other.'

This is Vernon Coleman's tenth book about cats.

Vernon Coleman is ageing rapidly and has become rather threadbare. If he were a cat he would have chunks bitten out of his ears and would now spend most of his time asleep in the airing cupboard. He is married to Donna Antoinette (also a cataholic) who

The first known photograph of the author in existence shows him clutching a cat to his chest.

not only grows younger and more beautiful by the day (although she does not have a picture in the attic) but who defies reality and the inevitable vicissitudes of a wicked world by constantly becoming gentler and more loving.